The Law and the Diving Professional

The Law and the Diving Professional

Written by: E. Steven Coren, J.D.

Edited by: Alex Brylske

Contributing Author and Consultant:
Neil Dougherty, Ed.D.

Additional Consultants: C. Craig Carlson,
Richard Goodman, Al Hornsby

Legal Research: Elliot Harrison

Assistant Editors: Mary Ellen Beveridge, Tonya Szabo

Design and Production: Jean Kester, Joy Lobell Zuehls

Typography: Don Osborne, Dail Schroeder

Typists: Lois Corcoran, Rita McBride, Marie Sulkey

Published by PADI

DISCLAIMER

This text was prepared, in cooperation with other legal experts, by an attorney who is qualified to practice in the state of Massachusetts. The book is intended to give you a basic understanding of some of the legal issues and principles that are, or should be, of concern to you. The book is not intended to be a definitive statement of the law or liability within your state, or to apply specifically to you in any particular situation. If you have specific questions or need specific legal advice, you should contact an attorney licensed to practice in your state.

Published by PADI, 1243 East Warner Avenue, Santa Ana, California 92705.

Printed in the United States of America.

9 8 7 6 5 4 3

Foreword

You are about to explore some important areas that concern legal liability in the field of recreational scuba-diving instruction and related activities. While these legal aspects are dealt with primarily from the instructor's perspective, much of this information also applies to recreational scuba retailers, repairers or manufacturers of scuba equipment, dive-boat operators, and owners of property and swimming pools in which scuba instruction takes place.

Normally, not much time is spent thinking about legal matters that relate to diving until *after* an incident having legal concerns occurs. Unfortunately, in some instances, ignorance of even the most elementary legal principles may result in very severe and costly consequences. Acquiring some basic knowledge can help you be *forearmed and forewarned* as to appropriate legal obligations and consequences. Preventive legal maintenance is just like preventive health care or preventive engine maintenance. The time taken to minimize your potential liability and to guard against the risks of liability may well be worthwhile.

In this manual, we will discuss several critically important issues, many of which have never been addressed in terms that are understandable to the layman. Hopefully, this comprehensive knowledge of the proper conduct that is required by the law will increase your awareness and ability to anticipate, guard against and minimize the risk of liability.

Finally, this manual was written with every member of the diving industry in mind. In such a highly regulated society, all activity is based on principles of legal rights and responsibilities. Ignorance of the law will not be any protection. Being informed will not only be advantageous, but the time you spend learning about the law will be invaluable in anticipating and preventing legal problems.

Biographical Sketches

Steve Coren

Steve Coren is an author, teacher and practicing attorney who specializes in civil litigation. Coren is a member of the Massachusetts bar, the Massachusetts Academy of Trial Attorneys, and is qualified to practice before the U.S. District Court and Court of Appeals. During his distinguished career, Steve has served as a Special Assistant Attorney General, and has devoted himself to a number of legal-education projects. Coren has served as a consultant in the field of legal education to various public television programs. In 1984, Steve was presented a distinguished service award from the Massachusetts Association for Law-Related Education.

Steve is also no stranger to the diving world. Coren has represented numerous New England-based diving organizations on various legal matters. As a PADI Instructor since 1976, he has spoken at many instructor-training programs on the topic of the legal liability of diver education. Coren is a member of the New England Aquarium Dive Team Steve dedicates this work to his mother and father, Alice and Simon Coren.

Neil Dougherty

Dr. Neil Dougherty is one of the foremost experts in the field of liability and risk management of recreational instruction. He is currently the Director of the School of Health Sciences at Rutgers University, and he is the President of the National Association of Physical Education in Higher Education. Neil has authored several books on both teaching *and* management principles for sports and recreational activities. In addition to teaching and writing, Neil serves as a legal consultant and speaker on legal issues that relate to teaching recreational activities.

Table of Contents

Introduction

Based on current accident statistics, it is accurate to state that recreational diving is a safe sport. Improvements in equipment, emphasis on proper and thorough training, and the concern of diving organizations for the sport have all contributed to minimizing the inherent risks in diving. However, the very nature of scuba diving contains the potential risk of injury and, as in most other recreational activities, that potential risk is occasionally realized. An important difference between scuba diving and most other sports is the potential severity and degree of injury. No matter how small the risk of injury, if an injury does occur, it has the potential to be serious.

A human being becomes a diver when he leaves the oxygen-based atmosphere and enters into a potentially hostile environment. The diver is then dependent on scuba gear and subject to the risks of loss of air, changes in physiology caused by increased pressures and increased absorption of nitrogen and other gases.

How does the law apply when something goes wrong and injury occurs? If someone is severely injured, can there be compensation for the injuries? How does the instructor know what to do to avoid acts that may incur liability for a student's injury? These questions are of great importance to anyone connected with the sport of scuba diving. Along with the risks inherent in the sport, it must also be remembered that society has become "litigation-conscious." If an injury occurs, it is more likely than not that someone will be sued, and a jury or judge will have to make decisions of tremendous consequence. It is important, therefore, to be familiar with some principles of law in this area. The law creates certain obligations and standards against which conduct is judged. Ignorance of the law will not shield us from the legal consequences of our acts. Some knowledge of the law will provide the foresight and ability needed to better understand the consequences of our acts. Thus, we will become better equipped in protecting ourselves from liability for another's injuries.

There is no one set of federal or state laws or regulations governing scuba instruction, scuba equipment or dive charters. Yet, almost every aspect of instruction, sales, leasing and charters involve legal relationships that create varied legal obligations and consequences. Any act, no matter how well-intentioned, can trigger unexpected consequences involving laws and regulations. Recreational scuba involves a number of legal considerations — including instructor liability, negligence, warranties, sales, releases, rentals, contracts and liability insurance. Every scuba lesson, purchase or rental of equipment, or dive charter has potential legal consequences.

Of particular significance in our discussion of the lega

aspects of diving is the role of the instructor. The instructor introduces students to the sport of scuba diving, and from this relationship flows the use and enjoyment of scuba equipment, dive-boat charters, dive trips, scuba sales and rentals. The instructor-student relationship brings into play all of the elements of the law of *civil liability* or *negligence.* Civil liability is an area that illustrates the care owed by the instructor for the safety of the students. A discussion of this area should be helpful for the instructor in learning how to minimize the risk of liability.

One

Negligence: Concepts and Definitions

Before exploring the intricacies of how the American legal system can affect scuba instruction and related activities, we must first establish a common base of knowledge. This is the purpose of section one. Primarily, most legal matters involving diving instruction center around the concept of *negligence.*

Our legal system is a codification of how individuals are expected to behave in relation to one another. Implied within this definition is that should someone not live up to this expectation, certain consequences will result. Because of the specialized knowledge held by the instructor and the potential for injury to the student, the relationship between a diving instructor and his student is one of particular importance. How the law views this special relationship is the subject of this section.

Herein we will discuss a wide range of information

essential to understanding the laws of negligence. To begin, we will address extensively the concepts of *unreasonable risk, foreseeability* and *standard of care* to establish the precise legal definition of negligence.

Next, we will review the formula for establishing negligence. Within this formula, we will explore the concepts of *duty, breach of duty, causation and proximate cause,* and *damages.* As we shall see, all four components of the formula must be present to establish negligence.

Finally, we will consider the concepts of *comparative* and *contributory* negligence. In this discussion we will see how the law attempts to deal with situations in which the injured party is partly to blame for his own damage or injury. Critical to understanding this important aspect of negligence law is the concept of *assumption of risk,* which will be elaborated on both within this section and in latter sections also.

Negligence

How does the law determine when a person is responsible for injuries unintentionally caused to another person? This decision involves the principles of the law of *negligence.*

> A scuba instructor has taken a class of students to the ocean for their first open-water training dive. The instructor has provided tanks, regulators and pressure gauges. The instructor has mistakenly forgotten to fill one of the scuba tanks, and it contains only 200 psi of air. However, the pressure gauge attached to the tank is defective and always gives a reading of 2500 psi. Shortly after the dive begins, the student wearing this tank runs out of air in 25 feet of water and panics. The instructor releases the student's weight belt, inflates the student's vest to full capacity and, after watching the student head toward the surface, returns to the rest of the class still on the bottom. The student in trouble suffers a fatal embolism.

Is there fault on the part of the instructor? Was this fault the major cause of the student's fatality? If so, what conduct on the part of the instructor contributed to the injury? Could the instructor have prevented this situation? Should the instructor have anticipated these problems?

These questions represent the process by which the law determines whether a person has acted carelessly enough to be held liable for injuries resulting from such carelessness. This determination is what the law of negligence is all about. Negligence is only one of several types of civil wrongs, called *torts*. Torts include intentional civil wrongs, such as assault and battery, intentional injury or destruction to property, as well as other areas, such as libel, slander or nuisance. The case of a civil wrong is a private lawsuit in which the injured person sues the person causing the injury for money damages (a criminal wrong, or crime, is one in which the state prosecutes the wrongdoer).

Negligence is concerned with unintentional fault or carelessness resulting in injury. In other words, *negligence deals with "avoidable accidents" that should have been anticipated and prevented by taking reasonable precautions.*

The intent of the negligent person in a case of negligence is irrelevant in determining responsibility. Even though no harm may be intended, a person is still negligent if such conduct was careless and would foreseeably cause harm. Thus, negligence operates on a standard of carelessness or lack of foresight. A person may act in a manner thought acceptable in a given situation, yet the law may still find negligence if the conduct doesn't measure up to a minimum standard of reasonable or due care. Therefore, the law is actually saying we should have known better when our conduct is found to be negligent.

The law of negligence is concerned with our conduct, not our state of mind. If our conduct doesn't conform to what the law demands, it is negligent regardless of whether the conduct stemmed from anger, stupidity, forgetfulness, thoughtlessness, carelessness or ignorance.

Unreasonable Risk and Foreseeability

The standard of conduct of negligence, against which a person's acts are measured, involves the creation of an *unreasonable risk* of harm to others. The key word is *unreasonable.* It would be ridiculous for a law to require absolute responsibility for *all* the consequences of *all* acts *all* times. If this were so, no one would ever step out the front door of his home again for fear of the consequences of anything he did. The law of negligence comes into play only when conduct is deemed as creating an unreasonable risk of harm, not simply any risk of harm. Everyone has a responsibility or "duty" to act reasonably toward others, thereby avoiding the creation of an unreasonable risk of harm. Accidents can happen, but from a legal standpoint they are excusable only if there is no unreasonable conduct involved. Conduct that falls below the required standard of conduct in a given situation will be considered negligent conduct if it creates an unreasonable risk of harm to others, and such risk is realized in terms of injury to another. The law of negligence is applied at the point where injuries result from conduct that created an unreasonable risk of harm.

So, how does the law of negligence decide when conduct has created an unreasonable risk of harm? Unreasonable risk of harm is determined through the concepts of *foreseeability, the exercise of reasonable precautions* and *the use of due care.*

The concept of foreseeability asks whether the harmful consequences of a person's conduct should have been foreseeable or anticipated. Negligence is not concerned with how well-meaning the person was at the time of the wrongful conduct. Thus, a person may be found negligent — even if that person felt that he had considered all the consequences of his conduct.

If an unreasonable risk of harm is deemed to be foreseeable as a result of a person's conduct, then reasonable precautions must be taken to guard against this foreseeable unreasonable risk of harm. These precautions need only be reasonable. The law does not require a person to have ESP or to take every precaution in the world regardless of cost or circumstance. The reverse of this concept is also true. A person is not negligent if an unreasonable risk of harm is foreseen, reasonable precautions are taken to guard against the harm, yet, harmful consequences occur. If a person has acted reasonably in the eyes of the law, then there can be no responsibility if injury still results. Thus, the law does not hold us absolutely responsible for all the consequences of our acts under any circumstance. There exists liability only when conduct creates an unreasonable risk of harm that should have been foreseen and reasonably guarded against. If injury results from failure to foresee consequences that should have been anticipated, then there is liability.

The failure to reasonably foresee the consequences of acts that create an unreasonable risk of harm may be characterized as a *failure to use due care.*

The following examples should help to illustrate these principles:

A scuba instructor is operating a motorboat carrying scuba students to a training-dive site. As the boat enters a cove, the instructor suffers a heart attack, the boat goes out of control hitting a rock and some of the passengers are injured. The instructor has never experienced any heart-related problems before and had recently undergone a routine medical examination that found the instructor to be in excellent health.

In this example, there is no negligence. No unreasonable risk of harm was created by the instructor that could be held to have been foreseeable. There was no reason or circumstance from which to anticipate that a heart attack might occur. There must always be some reason to anticipate harmful consequences from a particular conduct.

Thus, we must guard against only unreasonable risks of harm that can be reasonably anticipated, as opposed to all risks of harm, no matter how remote. For instance, it could be argued that we all run the remote risk of having a sudden heart attack, no matter how unlikely it may be. To guard against this, every person who is operating a motorboat, automobile, airplane and so on, should always be accompanied by another person. However, this risk is too remote, and there is no reason to anticipate this risk without some prior indication of such a problem. Therefore, it cannot be said that an unreasonable risk of harm has been created that should have been foreseen.

A scuba instructor is operating a motorboat carrying scuba students to a training-dive site. As the boat enters a cove, the instructor passes out, the boat goes out of control hitting a rock and some of the passengers are injured. The instructor had been experiencing sudden blackouts daily for several weeks prior to the accident.

Compare this example to the circumstances outlined in the previous example. Is there a significant difference? Yes. The instructor in this example would probably be found negligent.

Here, an unreasonable risk of harm (loss of control of the boat) was created by the instructor's negligent conduct (operating a boat with the knowledge that he is subject to sudden blackouts). The knowledge of the continued reoccurrence of such spells made it likely, or foreseeable, that a spell could occur while operating a boat, which could foreseeably result in loss of control of the boat. This certainly creates an unreasonable risk of harm, and the consequence of this risk should have been foreseen or anticipated by the instructor. Further, given the foreseeability of such consequences, the instructor did not take any reasonable precautions to guard against the unreasonable risk of harm, such as having an experienced person present in the boat to take over the helm.

Now let's take a look at another situation involving consequences that should have been foreseen but were ignored and resulted in severe harm.

> Jim is on a dive with seven other divers. They descend in pairs in full wet suits and scuba to investigate a wreck. Visibility is murky and limited to eight feet. Jim's weight belt has a defective buckle that will not hold the weight belt together. Jim knows this, and for his last few dives he has twisted the ends of the belt together. As Jim swims with his dive buddy, he is careful to never be directly above his buddy in case the weight belt lets go. However, Jim's weight belt does come apart and slips off and down. Unknown to Jim, one of the other divers is ten feet below him, and Jim's weight belt strikes the diver in the face, breaking the diver's mask and knocking the mouthpiece of the regulator out of the diver's mouth. The diver is stunned and severely injured.

In this example, Jim's conduct created an unreasonable risk of harm. However, Jim may argue that he foresaw the consequences of the belt letting go and took precautions against the weight belt injuring the only diver Jim expected to be near him, which was his dive buddy. Was it reasonably foreseeable that a diver other than Jim's buddy could be injured? Did Jim use reasonable or due care in the circumstances? Jim probably would be held to have foreseen this consequence. Jim foresaw one type of consequence of his conduct but should also have foreseen another consequence that he did not. It was likely, or foreseeable, that, with six other divers around in poor visibility, an unseen diver could be underneath Jim at a time when the weight belt might slip. Therefore, Jim should have foreseen the consequences and did not take any reasonable precautions to guard against such an occurrence.

This example also illustrates the important principle that the concept of foreseeability does not mean a person has to foresee the consequences in the exact manner and result in which they occur to be found negligent. A person is negligent when the harm resulting was of a generally foreseeable nature, even though an actual specific injury and its nature of occurrence may not have been foreseen. This principle is further illustrated in the next example.

> A scuba instructor arrives at an open-water dive site to conduct a certification dive. The students are standing in a group waiting for their instructor. Intent on impressing the class, the instructor removes a heavy bag of dive gear from his car with one hand and casually tosses the gear bag in the direction of the students, yelling "Catch." The bag strikes one of the students, Kathy, in the stomach. Kathy is knocked down but gets right up and appears unhurt. However, Kathy has recently had her appendix out, and the gear bag struck her in the exact area where she had stitches from the operation. A short while later, Kathy feels increasing pain and experiences bleeding in her abdominal area. Kathy is taken to a hospital. Infection sets in, and Kathy is in the hospital for a week.

The instructor's conduct in this example is negligent. His act created an unreasonable risk of harm. What consequences are foreseeable here? Kathy was knocked to the ground but suffered no apparent injury. That consequence was certainly foreseeable. However, the further consequences that followed the tossing of the bag seem so unpredictable and improbable. The instructor was unaware of Kathy's condition. A person may be tempted to feel that the specific consequences to Kathy were unforeseeable. Should the instructor be responsible for such a disastrous coincidence arising out of seemingly minor horseplay? The answer is yes. The instructor did not have to foresee the exact consequences that occurred. He is merely held to foresee the general nature of the probable consequences of the act, even though the specific results seem disproportionately severe in comparison to the minor consequences the instructor might have foreseen to be the result of the horseplay. Thus, the specific harm need not be anticipated in order to be liable as long as the general risk of harm created was foreseeable, and the ultimate specific harm was a natural and probable result of the original negligent act. This includes aggravation of a preexisting infirmity as occurred here.

Remember also that negligence is not concerned with what the actor intended. The instructor might have felt that the worst that could happen would be that someone may be knocked harmlessly to the ground. The instructor did not intend nor desire that such a chain of events would happen. As we have seen, the law of negligence is concerned not with the instructor's state of mind but with his acts and with what he should have foreseen. Kathy's injuries are included as a natural and probable consequence of the instructor's negligence.

Next, let's examine an example of conduct creating an unreasonable risk of harm in which resulting injuries are *not* the natural and probable consequences of the conduct, and are therefore not forseeable.

> A scuba instructor takes a class on an open-water certification dive. The instructor has not set up a dive flag, which is a violation of state law. While the class is on the surface of the water, a small airplane flying nearby runs out of fuel, lands

on the water on top of the class and severely injures a student. There is no airport around for many miles, and the site of the class was not in any airplane flight path.

As will be explained later, violation of a law may be evidence of negligent conduct where not obeying a law designed to protect people in a certain situation creates an unreasonable risk of harm. Let's assume this is the case here, and the instructor's conduct has created such a risk of harm. However, dive-flag laws are designed to protect divers from boat traffic. Was the harm that occurred in this example the natural and probable consequence of the instructor's conduct? In other words, was this risk of harm foreseeable? The answer is no. Being struck by an airplane is in no way a foreseeable consequence of failure to display a dive flag. Though the instructor was negligent in failing to display a dive flag, the harm was not the natural and probable result of the instructor's negligent conduct.

In summary, negligence is conduct that creates an unreasonable risk of harm that was reasonably foreseeable and for which reasonable precautions should have been taken. Notice the words *reasonable* and *unreasonable*. The principles of negligence employ a concept of reasonableness. Thus, we must only guard against unreasonable risks of harm, not all risks, no matter how remote. These risks of harm must have been reasonably foreseeable; meaning we are not expected to predict the future but only to anticipate unreasonable risks that are judged foreseeable. Precautions against such risk of harm need only be reasonable in nature, depending on the circumstances.

Standard of Care

One further principle of negligence needs to be explored.

How does the law determine the amount of reasonable care owed by a person in order to judge whether the conduct of that person was negligent? Since the law judges our conduct objectively, without regard to our intent, there has to be some consistent standard against which conduct is measured.

The law has developed such a standard. Conduct is measured against a fictitious, ideal person who always uses due care and always acts prudently in any circumstance. This is the RPP, or *reasonably prudent person.*

The RPP standard is applied in any given case and compared to the conduct of the person who is charged with being negligent. (In a lawsuit, the person claiming to be injured is called the plaintiff, and the person charged with being negligent is called the defendant. For easier reference, these terms will be used in differentiating between the person injured and the person negligently causing the injury.) If the defendant's conduct fails to conform to what the RPP would have done in the same situation, then the defendant is negligent.

The RPP's conduct in every situation will conform to the appropriate standard of due care, since the RPP is infallible in his ability to always act reasonably and to never create unreasonable risks of harm.

What kind of person is the RPP? The RPP is a composite person who possesses all the knowledge of ordinary experience, i.e., that fire burns, that shouting "Fire!" in a crowded cinema will cause a panic, and so on. The RPP never fails in taking note of his immediate environment and thereby always chooses courses of conduct that will not act on, or combine with, immediate environmental circumstance to create unreasonable risks of harm.

When the RPP is compared to a defendant, the RPP

takes on the mental and physical characteristics of the defendant so that the comparison is fair. The RPP is placed in our shoes, so to speak. Thus, the RPP is given any particular superior mental or physical abilities the defendant may actually possess, in addition to any mental or physical deficiencies.

This concept of the RPP also applies to scuba instructors. If an instructor's conduct in a particular instance is questioned, it will be measured against what the RPP would have done in the same circumstances. Since the instructor possesses superior knowledge and skill in a given area, the RPP will also assume this knowledge and skill. The RPP will *not*, however, assume subjective qualities of temperament, such as bad judgment, stupidity, arrogance, genius, incompetence or ignorance. Thus, the RPP, when compared to a scuba instructor, will take on the qualities of the *reasonably prudent scuba instructor,* or the RPSI. An instructor is not measured against the best instructors in the field, nor the worst — merely the reasonably prudent scuba instructor in good standing and possessed of the knowledge of the most recent improvements and changes in the field of scuba instruction.

How do we know how the RPSI will act in a given situation? The RPSI's conduct is based on a composite of sources consisting of training standards, state and municipal laws, publications and expert opinion. From all of these sources, it is possible to determine a pattern of conduct that would be considered reasonable and prudent under the circumstances. If the instructor's conduct falls short of the conduct of the RPSI, then the instructor would most likely be negligent.

We'll now begin to experience a more practical application of the field of negligence to scuba instruction and other related areas. It isn't necessary at this point of discussion to understand completely all the principles that were just explained. It will take some thought, some time and some repetition. It's only important to grasp the general framework of how the law has established a standard by which conduct is judged. It should now be understood that seemingly proper conduct may be found deficient under legal scrutiny. With this knowledge, we can develop some additional ability to assess our conduct in terms of legal expectations and to conduct our instructional activities with more confidence.

The Formula Of Negligence

There is a practical formula that can be used to reduce the principles of negligence to their basic stages. It is used by lawyers and courts in determining whether a case of negligence exists. A lawyer sifts through the facts, applies the formula and determines whether these facts fulfill, more or less, the minimum legal requirements needed to support a lawsuit for negligence. The formula consists of:

1. A duty
2. A breach of the duty
3. Causation and proximate cause
4. Damages

These four parts of the formula are based on the general principles discussed in the previous section. If a person goes to a lawyer with a possible case of negligence, the lawyer must be able to determine that each part of the formula is sustained by the facts. The lawyer must subsequently convince a court of the merit of the cause of action by proving that each and every part of the formula is supported by the evidence.

Every part of the formula must be proved by the facts to win, not just two or three out of the four parts. As each part of the formula is discussed, the terms *plaintiff* and *defendant* will be used. As described previously, a plainti is an individual or organization that brings suit in court for damages. A defendant is the person or organization against whom the lawsuit is brought and from whom dam ages are sought. All plaintiffs and defendants named in a lawsuit (whether individuals, companies or other organizations) are *parties* to the lawsuit.

Let's examine this formula as it pertains to scuba instruction.

Duty

Negligent conduct is conduct that falls short of what a reasonably prudent person (RPP) would have done in the same circumstances and that brings about an injury. As explained previously, the RPP is a measure used to establish a standard against which actual conduct is judged. This standard, in the formula of negligence, is called the *duty of care.*

The duty of care is that amount of reasonable care owed to others that will not create an unreasonable risk o harm. In any given situation, there will be a particular du ty of care to refrain from acting negligently toward others

There are two major categories of duty. The first category is a general duty to act with reasonable care toward others so as not to create an unreasonable risk of harm. Each person owes this duty to every other person.

> A scuba diver is on a small boat filled with other scuba divers. There is very little room for movement, and the passengers are close together. Upon arrival at the dive site, the scuba diver swings a scuba tank onto his shoulder with the end of the tank projecting behind. The diver then turns around without looking or announcing his intention, and the projecting end strikes another diver in the head.

In this example, the scuba diver had a duty to act in a way that would not create an unreasonable risk of harm to others. Did the diver's conduct fall below this standard of care? Did the diver's actions create an unreasonable risk of harm? In this situation, the scuba diver violated or breached the duty to act with reasonable care. The scuba diver's conduct was unreasonable, given the circumstances. The diver was aware of the crowded conditions. It was foreseeable that, without taking the precaution of warning the other passengers or at least looking to see if there was safe clearance, swinging a tank in such conditions was likely to injure someone.

This general duty of care is concerned with acts that are negligent. This duty does not, however, include a failure to act (omission) if there is no obligation to act. For instance, in coming upon a person in distress, there is no duty to act to aid that person, and it is not negligent to fail to act (assuming there was no obligation to care for that person's safety). However, if a person's conduct causes a victim to be put in a perilous situation, then there is a duty to rescue and there is also liability to anyone else who is injured while attempting to rescue the victim. Further, once a rescue is undertaken, a duty of care is owed to the victim not to worsen the victim's circumstances.

A duty of care in any given circumstance may be defined by any number of sources. Laws, traffic ordinances, rules of the road, navigational rules or regulations that apply to a certain situation may create a standard of conduct that, if violated, results in negligence.

> A boat operator enters a harbor area in a motorboat at night without navigation lights. Another boat collides with the unlit boat.

The unlit boat was in violation of navigation rules. This may constitute negligent conduct or evidence of negligent conduct. If this conduct tended to cause the accident, then the operator of the unlit boat is liable for the damages.

Duty and Legal Relationship

Another major category of duty arises out of a legal relationship between persons. In these situations, there exist positive duties to act, and there can be liability for failing to do something. Examples of such relationships are doctor-patient, lawyer-client, teacher-student, accountant-client, landlord-tenant, landowner-invitee and many others. Specific duties of care that set standards of conduct have been developed by statutes and court decisions by reason of these relationships.

This type of duty calling for specific standards of care involves much of the scuba-diving industry, where many legal relationships exist. There are particular duties of care owed by a scuba-equipment manufacturer or retailer to a purchaser, by a lessor (renter) of scuba equipment to lessee (someone who rents), by a scuba equipment repairer to a customer and by a dive-charter-boat owner or operator to passengers. These relationships will be covered in latter sections.

A scuba instructor-student situation is a legal relationship, and this relationship calls for specific duties of care on the part of the instructor. It is important to realize that the scuba instructor owes a degree of care to his students in light of the inherent risks of scuba diving, since scuba students justifiably rely on the instructor for their protection and safety. Scuba instructors must adhere to a carefully prudent standard of instructional conduct for several reasons:

1. Sport diving is a potentially hazardous activity.
2. A scuba instructor possesses superior knowledge and skill.
3. A student must rely on the instructor for knowledge, protection and reasonable safety

Scuba instruction places responsibilities with substantial consequence on the instructor. Scuba diving is a relatively safe sport for the competent and safety-conscious diver, but there are some inherent risks that loom large for the beginning scuba student. During a scuba course, the student must rely completely on the instructor for proper instruction. The student must place his confidence completely in the instructor for his reasonable safety while in the water under the instructor's care. The student must also assume that the instructor possesses reasonable competence and the required amount of specialized knowledge and teaching ability to produce a competent and able scuba diver. The instructor is attributed superior abilities by students due to the instructor's superior position. This fact is particularly significant when remembering the substantial reliance an entry-level student must place on the instructor when in the water. Hence, the superiority of position demands a correspondingly careful duty of care on the part of the scuba instructor.

The Duty of Care Defined

It is impossible to predict the proper duty that is owed to a student in any particular situation involving injury to a student. Each situation has its own innumerable factors to be considered. However, there are some general standards against which an instructor's conduct in a situation will be measured. These standards help define the duty of care owed by a scuba instructor. The following areas are suggestive of such standards:

1. A scuba instructor should possess and use that degree of knowledge, ability and skill usually possessed by competent instructors in the field of scuba instruction.

2. A scuba instructor's conduct will be measured against the commonly accepted standards of instruction of national diving-instruction organizations.
3. A scuba instructor must exercise that same degree of care that would be exercised by a reasonably prudent scuba instructor (RPSI) in the same situation when considering the current state of advancement of the profession.

To satisfy this duty of teaching a student properly and keeping the student safe from any unreasonable risk, an instructor must be concerned with every aspect of a scuba course.

Duty and the Law — There are several sources that define the duty of care owed by a scuba instructor to scuba students. One area consists of laws — including federal, state and municipal laws — as well as regulations. Navigation laws and dive-flag laws are common examples. A law sets forth a standard of conduct that, if disobeyed, may give rise to liability for negligence. Thus, an instructor should be familiar and comply with state and local laws that may pertain to scuba or boating activities. If such a law is violated, and this violation causes injury to a scuba student, then this violation may create liability on the part of the instructor.

Duty and Adherence to Training Standards — Another area that defines an instructor's duty of care is the instructional standards of national instructional agencies, such as PADI. Agencies establish specific standards of instruction, course content, sequence and assessment of individual skills. An instructor must comply with the standards of any agency through which the instructor certifies. These agency standards provide accepted standards of conduct that help to determine the duty of care of an instructor in nearly any given situation. This concept is further defined as to different diving areas and climates, as one region may differ markedly from another in terms of climate, conditions, marine life and so on.

The importance of instructors following the standards of their instructional agencies cannot be overemphasized. *This is probably the most significant criterion against which an instructor's conduct can be measured.* An instructor should follow certification-agency requirements to the letter, with special care paid to safety procedures, such as student-to-instructor ratios, maximum open-water training depths, and constant instructor presence and attentiveness. PADI Standards and Procedures* is a good example of a detailed and safe scuba-course structure. These certification standards must, however, be used and followed for an instructor to be able to show that he has indeed carried out the duty of care owed to scuba students. There is really no excuse not to, and a lapse from such standards that results in student injury may cause serious legal consequences.

Duty and Court Decisions — A third area that is looked to in determining an instructor's duty of care is court decisions. A court decision based on a set of facts highly analogous to a scuba incident may be relied on as a precedent illuminating the duty owed in a scuba instructional incident. A jury hears the facts and decides, based on these facts, what a duty should be, and this decision establishes a guide for later cases.

*Refers to those standards and procedures detailed in the "Standards and Procedures" section of the PADI Instructor Manual.

When Duty Does Not Apply

It is important to remember that an instructor's duty of

care normally comes into play *only* between an instructo and his students. It should not apply to an instructor and other divers with whom the instructor happens to be div- ing when there is no instructor-student relationship.

> An instructor goes out on a boat dive with other divers. The instructor has no students along nor does the instructor have any connection with the organization of the trip. As the in- structor suits up for the first dive, the instructor sees that another diver is wearing a flotation device that has a tear in the bladder.

Does this instructor have a duty as an instructor to warn or prevent the other diver from using the defective flota- tion device? Is the instructor responsible if the other dive: is injured because the instructor failed to do anything? The answer to these concerns is that the instructor shoul« not be considered responsible to the other diver and should not be liable should an accident occur merely be- cause he is an instructor. There may exist a moral respon- sibility but not a legal responsibility. There is no legal rel\; tionship between the instructor and any other diver on the boat. If he is absent from any relationship, the instruc tor has no duty of care to the other divers to affirmatively act on their behalf. The instructor must only refrain from creating an unreasonable risk of harm to others, which did not occur in this example.

Breach of Duty

Now that the duty of care owed by a scuba instructor has been defined, the next part of the formula of negligence to be applied is whether a breach or violation of the duty of care has occurred. Did the instructor fail to conform to the required standard of care, thereby creating an unrea- sonable risk of harm?

An instructor's breach of duty may consist of either an *act* done that the reasonably prudent scuba instructor (RPSI) would not have done or the failure to do something that the RPSI would have done. The latter is termed an *omission.*

A breach of duty may be proved in several ways, examples of which are mentioned later, such as violation of a law, a certification standard, or court decisions that have ruled on similar conduct.

Violation of a law that results in harm that the law sought to prevent is evidence of a breach of duty. A particular law can create a standard of conduct or duty of care, and violation of this law can constitute a breach of duty. A law does not have to be concerned with scuba instruction. If such a law must be obeyed in the context of the instruction, then it can create a duty of care. A dive-flag law is a good example.

> A scuba instructor takes a class into the ocean for a certification-training dive. The instructor has neglected to display a dive flag or flags on the surface in violation of a state law. A boat strikes one of the students on the surface.

In violating this dive-flag law, the instructor has breached his duty of care to the students. The instructor is responsible (within reason) for the students' safety. Violation of a law that creates an unreasonable risk for the scuba students can constitute negligent conduct.

A breach of duty can also consist of failure to follow instructional standards. These expert standards define, more than any other source, what duty of care is owed to scuba students by an instructor. It is worth repeating that *an instructor should not deviate from these standards in any way that tends to reduce the care, vigilance and protection owed to scuba students as prescribed by such instruction standards.*

There can be situations involving instructor negligence in which no clear violation of law or training standards is involved. In these instances, expert testimony at a trial will be used to determine whether instructor conduct is negligent in a particular situation. An *expert* is a person whose credentials, qualifications and expertise in the field of recreational scuba instruction, if deemed sufficient by a court to qualify that person as an expert, entitle that person to give an opinion as to whether an instructor's conduct was proper or negligent in the circumstances. An expert may testify whether, in the context of a particular training standard, the instructor properly followed the standard and whether the failure, if any, to follow a standard was the cause of a scuba-instruction accident.

Instructor Judgment

In many instances, an instructor's judgment may be the subject of an expert's opinion.

> A scuba instructor takes several students into the ocean for their first open-water training dive. The students enter the water from a rocky shore. There is a strong wind, a strong undertow, three-foot waves and heavy surf at the shoreline. The water is cold. At the end of the dive, as the students attempt to exit the water, a student is injured on the rocks in the surf.

This example involves instructor judgment. Were the conditions unsuitable for scuba students with no prior open-water diving experience?

The important point to remember for an instructor is to use proper foresight and to always exercise judgment on the side of student safety. An instructor should exercise judgment only after considering all appropriate factors, such as environmental conditions, the physical and mental faculties and conditions of the students, and availability of teaching assistants. However, *judgments should always be consistent with training standards and instruction-safety standards*. These standards are designed to not only produce a properly trained entry-level scuba diver but are also an important protection for the instructor if they are followed. If an instructor clearly deviates from a certification standard, then the instructor is only decreasing the defendability of his teaching activities (in addition to potentially lessening the safety of his students).

If an instructor's conduct is considered negligent, this does not necessarily mean that the instructor is liable for injuries to a scuba student. There still remains another element in the negligence formula that must exist. The negligent conduct must have been the cause of the injury. There can be instances where conduct is negligent but is not the cause of the harm.

Proximate Cause

If a breach of duty by a scuba instructor exists, the formula of negligence requires another element to be proved. The harm to a scuba student must be shown to have been the natural and probable consequence of the instructor's negligent conduct. Put another way, *the injury must be the result of an unreasonable risk of harm that was a reasonably foreseeable consequence of the instructor's conduct.* The exact nature of the injury does not need to be anticipated. Proximate cause is present if it should have been foreseen or anticipated that the probable consequence of the negligent conduct would result in the same general kind of harm to anyone who was in the zone of danger created by the negligent conduct. Thus, foreseeability does not require predictability of the precise nature of the injury or of the exact manner of occurrence. It means that the instructor's conduct created a reasonably foreseeable risk of harm to all persons within a zone of danger created by the defendant's conduct. For example, two students may suffer harm simultaneously because of instructor negligence. Both their injuries and their manner of occurrence may be the natural and probable consequences of the defendant's conduct. To find proximate cause, it is only necessary that both injuries and their manner of occurrence be the natural and probable consequence of the defendant's conduct.

If an unreasonable risk of harm is foreseeable, then the instructor must take reasonable precautions to guard against any harmful consequences of such a risk. Precautions may consist of emphatic adherence to safety standards, warnings or actual physical actions taken in the circumstances, or a combination of these precautions. Environmental conditions and the physical and mental abilities (or lack of them) on the part of each student must be taken into consideration.

> An instructor takes some students into the ocean for a training dive. The water is cold, and there are waves. The instructor is aware that one student in particular has shown some discomfort and lack of confidence in the use of scuba equipment. The instructor has the students pair themselves into diving partners but keeps this particular student as his dive partner.

Under these hypothetical circumstances, this would be appropriate conduct by the instructor. Given the foreknowledge of this student's weaknesses, the instructor had reason to believe that this student might become distressed in open-water conditions and therefore took appropriate precautions. If there is reason to believe an unreasonable risk of harm may occur, then the instructor is in a position to anticipate it. This possibility means that such a risk is foreseeable. What if the instructor left this weak student paired with another student, and the weak student got into trouble and sustained injury? Given this foreseeable consequence and given the instructor's duty of care for student safety, the instructor's failure to take reasonable precautions may be considered the proximate cause of the injury.

> An instructor takes some students on an open-water certification dive in a cove. Submerged in the path of the entry and exit area just below the surface is the remains of a wooden pier, which has large nails protruding from it. This condition is known to the instructor. A student sustains a serious puncture wound during entry into the cove waters.

Did the presence of this sunken pier with protruding nails represent an unreasonable risk of harm to which the students were subjected by the instructor? Assuming the instructor's obligation for the safety of the students and the instructor's knowledge of the dangerous condition, was this harm foreseeable? What reasonable precautions should the instructor have taken to guard against the condition? Applying the formula of negligence, there is no question a duty of care was owed to the students to protect them from unreasonable risks of harm. It is arguable that the instructor breached this duty by having them dive in an area where they became exposed to an unknown hazard that was known to the instructor. This breach of duty was more likely than not the proximate cause of the injury, meaning it was foreseeable that a student might be harmed by the protruding nails. Thus, the instructor, having chosen the dive site, should have taken reasonable precautions, such as warning the students of the presence and location of the hazard and/or stationing himself at the hazard to ward off any students who came close to it.

Let's change one part of the second example. Suppose, instead of suffering a puncture wound, the student unknowingly suffered a tear in the air bladder of his flotation device. At the end of the dive, tired and cold, the student surfaces and inflates the flotation device. Because of the tear, the flotation device will not float the student on the surface, and the student suffers severe injury.

The question of proximate cause becomes more significant. Was this harm a natural and probable consequence of the instructor's breach of duty? It is more likely than not that the instructor's negligence was the proximate cause of the injury. It can be argued that a tear in the air bladder was a foreseeable consequence of the undisclosed underwater hazard, and the resulting type of injury was just as foreseeable.

As already emphasized, however, an instructor is not held to predict the future. An instructor is not absolutely responsible for all injury to scuba students. There must be an unreasonable risk created due to instructor negligence and this risk must have been foreseeable.

> A scuba student suffers a severe injury during a certification-training dive with no fault on the part of the instructor. The student is competently rescued, proper first-aid treatment is administered and hospital emergency transport is immediately summoned. However, despite appropriate rapid response of emergency transport, the student suffers permanent injury due to passage of time prior to arrival at a hospital.

In this example, if the student had received immediate medical care in a medical facility, the severity of injury might have been avoided. What precautions would this require on the part of the instructor? There is always the potential of some risk in scuba diving, and this can be anticipated. However, anticipating this risk would then require every scuba instructor to have at the dive site a doctor, medical equipment and possibly, a helicopter. These are impossible burdens and, therefore, are not considered to be reasonably necessary precautions. Assuming scuba students are properly apprised of the inherent risks of scuba diving and voluntarily assume these risks (as will be discussed later), then the instructor is only responsible for *unreasonable* risks created by his negligence where the consequences of such risks should have been foreseen by the instructor.

In order for such a risk to be foreseeable, the instructor must have some reason to anticipate this risk.

> An instructor takes a scuba class on a training dive in a quarry. The instructor has conducted prior dives at this site and has determined that no submerged hazards exist. Entry is conducted by a four-foot drop into the water. Unknown to the instructor, however, an automobile has been dumped into the quarry and lies unseen just below the surface of the entry point. Further, no automobiles or other large objects have ever been located in the quarry at this entry point before. A student entering the water strikes the automobile and is injured.

In this example, the risk of harm was not foreseeable because there were no facts or circumstances from which the instructor could have anticipated such a risk. Perhaps it would have been appropriate for the instructor or an assistant to enter the water first to make sure the entry point was safe. Legally, however, precautions must be taken only to protect against a foreseeable unreasonable risk.

Incidentally, this example raises an important issue of the instructor's duty of care. Part of the instructor's responsibility is to provide a reasonably safe and manageable diving environment for training dives. If the instructor considers conducting a student training dive in a new area, the instructor's duty would include obtaining necessary information about the conditions of this new dive site. The nature of tides, currents, entries, exits, underwater topography and any hazards particular to this site should be determined in advance. Common sense should make this obvious, since any adverse conditions could create an unreasonable risk of harm to scuba students.

It is important to understand that the law places a burden on scuba instructors to anticipate the consequences of their acts (or failures to act) under the circumstances. This foreseeability element of the formula of negligence means, simply, foresight. A well-planned scuba course should be structured to anticipate and guard against any unreasonable risks. If reasonable precautions are taken in all reasonably foreseeable circumstances, then the instructor has properly fulfilled his duty of care to scuba students.

One further aspect of proximate cause worthy of discussion in the context of scuba instruction is intervening causes. A condition of unreasonable risk can be created that, by itself, will not result in harm but that can result in harm when acted upon by an intervening cause.

> A heavy ladder is left propped against the front of a dive store. The ladder is not secured to the building. A wind springs up and causes the ladder to topple over onto a customer walking out of the dive store.

In this example, an unreasonable risk of harm is created by leaving an unattended and unsecured ladder in an area where the public is invited. Is it foreseeable that something such as wind could topple the ladder? Common sense and basic experience should indicate that such an occurrence is not unexpected. This consequence should have been foreseeable.

Suppose that in our example some children accidently knocked the ladder over onto the customer. Was this negligent creation of an unreasonable risk (leaving the ladder unattended in a publicly traveled area) the proximate cause of the harm? The issue is whether the childrens' acts were a foreseeable intervening cause. If the dive-store owner had prior reason to believe children played around the dive store, then there is proximate cause. Knowledge of the playful and mischievous nature of most children is a matter of common sense. This means that in certain circumstances, negligence of other persons, if combined with a person's own negligence, should be foreseeable. This would then require reasonable precautions to be taken. Once again, the use of foresight, good judgment and common sense should prevent any unreasonable risks from arising in the first place.

Damages

The fourth and last element of the formula of negligence is *damage*. There must be some legally recognizable injury to a victim for damages to be recoverable. Injury can include physical injury/damage to property. Usually fright or emotional upset, without some accompanying physical injury, is not enough for a personal injury lawsuit. There must be some physical injury, no matter how slight. Where actual personal injury is shown, tort law seeks to compensate the victim monetarily for injuries and other attendant loss. This compensation is not a penalty placed upon the defendant, but is rather an attempt to make the injured person "whole." Obviously this cannot be done where injury results in permanent disability. All the law can do is to award a monetary result to fairly compensate the victim for all legally recognizable loss in terms of present and future consequences. This is called *compensatory damages.*

A damage award can consist of several components.

Medical expenses, lost wages during incapacity and pain and suffering (physical and emotional) make up the usua items of recovery. Pain and suffering generally comprise the largest monetary part of an award.

Permanent injuries are also compensable. In additio to the components listed above, anticipated future medical expenses, anticipated future lost wages/future loss of earning capacity are recoverable. Permanent scarring or disfigurement is recoverable. Permanent physical disabili ty, such as paralysis or loss of range of motion in a joint o limb is also recoverable.

If death is caused by negligence, it is called *wrongful death.* The estate of the deceased may recover a damage award consisting of funeral expenses, pain and suffering the victim suffered prior to death, medical expenses, loss of future earnings and loss of support, comfort and companionship by a spouse and children. State laws differ as to what losses are recoverable.

In the event of property damage, the fair market value of the property at the time of the damages is compensable.

This brief discussion is sufficient to give a general ide of the legal concept of damages. Hopefully, by gaining a better understanding of the consequences of instructiona conduct as shown in the preceding discussions, an instru tor need never have to know more about the concept of damages.

Comparative and Contributory Negligence

The principles of negligence establish a standard of conduct against which the acts or omissions of a scuba instructor are measured. The preceding discussion has shown that the law requires an affirmative duty of care on the part of an instructor toward his scuba students.

In any accident resulting from negligence, however, the conduct of the injured person is also subject to scrutiny. If the conduct of the injured person contributed in part to his own injuries, then the victim is considered *comparatively* or *contributorily* negligent.

A victim can, to some extent, be at fault in contributing to his own injury by exposing himself to an unreasonable risk that would have been apparent to the RPP.

> A scuba diver snorkels out from shore and descends on scuba in the ocean. The diver has a dive flag on the surface. As the diver runs low on air, he begins an ascent to the surface. As the diver surfaces, he is 200 feet from the dive flag and is struck by a motorboat being driven at a fast speed by an intoxicated operator. A state law requires a diver to display a dive flag within 100 feet of a diver on the surface.

Assume the diver brings an action of negligence against the boat operator. There appears to be negligence on the part of the operator. The operator was intoxicated and operated a boat at excessive speed in an area where a dive flag indicated that scuba divers were in the area. This conduct seems to fall below that expected of an RPP in the same circumstances. However, what is significant about the diver's conduct? The diver surfaced beyond the 100-foot radius of the flag. This action by the diver in violation of the law that was designed to protect against this risk of harm is evidence of contributory or comparative negligence. The diver's acts fell below that standard of conduct established by the dive-flag law.

> Two persons rent equipment from a dive store and go diving. Both divers have quick-release buckles on the body straps of the equipment and know they are quick-release buckle systems. They do *not* know, however, how to use the quick-

release buckles, so they tie all the straps on as best as they can. While under water, the victim intentionally or inadvertently removes his regulator mouthpiece and then panics. He tries unsuccessfully to remove his tank and other equipment that is weighing him down. The other diver tries to assist the victim by attempting to hand the victim back his regulator mouthpiece, but the victim, apparently because of panic, does not accept it. The victim drowns. The victim's estate sues the dive store for negligence in failing to provide a neck strap to hold the regulator mouthpiece near the victim's mouth.

This example is based on an actual case. The victim (plaintiff) lost the case because the court found that the victim's conduct contributed to his own death. The victim was contributorily negligent and his estate could not recover. The facts from the case are unclear as to the nature of the quick-release buckles, and exactly which type of equipment straps were tied. In any event, it is clear that the victim's conduct, in tying straps together and being unfamiliar in dealing properly with retrieval of a lost mouthpiece, contributed substantially to his own death. The dive store was not liable.

This case also demonstrates another principle of contributory negligence. Traditional negligence law held that if the plaintiff in a case was contributorily negligent in the slightest degree, then the plaintiff could not recover. The somewhat harsh nature of this rule has been changed in a great many states by adopting the concept of *comparative negligence.* This means that a plaintiff who is contributorily negligent is not prevented from recovering damages. Instead, the amount of negligence on the part of the plaintiff, if any, and on the part of the defendant is assigned a percentage figure by the jury, based on 100%. The plaintiff's monetary award is subsequently reduced proportionately by the percentage of negligence assessed, if any, on the part of the plaintiff. For instance, assume that a plaintiff is awarded $100,000 for injuries caused by a defendant's negligence. The plaintiff has been found to have been 20% comparatively negligent due to his own negligent conduct (the defendant, therefore, being 80% negligent). The plaintiff will then have deducted from the damage award a sum of money equal to 20%, which in this case would be 20% of $100,000 or $20,000. Thus the plaintiff would get $80,000. For the plaintiff to recover any damages, comparative-negligence laws in most states require that a plaintiff be *less* than 50% or 51% comparatively negligent, depending on the law of each particular state that has such a law. The trend to adopt comparative-negligence laws is growing, and it is likely that all states will eventually adopt such a law.

Assumption of Risk

A brief discussion of the principle of *assumption of risk* is of some interest. We need only discuss it briefly because many of the states that have adopted comparative negligence laws have abolished assumption of risk as a defense in a negligence case. In some states, however, it is still a valid and complete defense.

Assumption of risk occurs when a plaintiff encounters, accepts and subjects himself to a risk of harm created or maintained by the defendant. Essentially, the plaintiff is consenting to accept this risk, relieving the defendant of legal responsibility. For this defense to be successful, it must be shown that the plaintiff knew of and understood the nature of the risk and that the plaintiff's choice to incur this risk was freely and voluntarily made.

There is no assumption of the risk when the plaintiff is ignorant of a risky activity or condition. Further, the plaintiff must not only be aware of the facts that create the danger, but must also understand and appreciate the danger itself. Also, where a plaintiff is aware of and appreciates the nature of one risk, the plaintiff does not necessarily assume another risk of which he is unaware.

If a risk that any reasonably ordinary person of the same age, background, education and common experience as the plaintiff would appreciate and understand causes injury, the plaintiff will not be able to claim a lack of understanding or appreciation of such risk.

An assumption of the risk situation occurs when a plaintiff enters into some kind of legal relationship with the defendant, knowing that the defendant will not protect him against certain risks or negligent acts or conditions known and understood by the plaintiff. Thus, the plaintiff is consenting to incur the risk of a negligent act or condition.

The sport of scuba diving, whether in the context of an instructional class or recreational diving, contains some inherent risks. Water depth; limited visibility; cold, adverse weather conditions; dangerous marine life; equipment malfunction; decompression limits; dive-partner separation; or diving under the influence of alcohol or drugs all represent risks of harm that may potentially be realized.

If a risk is recognized, understood and appreciated by a plaintiff, and the plaintiff goes ahead with an activity supervised by a defendant involving such a risk, then a plaintiff can be said to have assumed the risk. This implication means there was no advanced, specific agreement reached in which the plaintiff was advised of any risks and formally agreed to accept them. By merely encountering a risk where it is reasonable to believe such a risk would be understood by the plaintiff, it may be presumed the plaintiff voluntarily consented to assume the risk.

In the context of scuba-diving instruction, it cannot be assumed that an entry-level dive student will understand all of the risks that may be encountered in scuba diving. It is important that such students be informed of these risks ahead of time so that they will be able to understand, appreciate and voluntarily assume these risks. This may be done by an oral or written expression of such risks prior to initiating any water activities. A written statement is preferable, since it may be preserved as a record of the nature of such risks and of the students' comprehension and voluntary assumption of such risks.

PADI has taken a significant step in this area with its Standard Safe Diving Practices Statement of Understanding form. This document sets out the diving conduct necessary for safe diving practices. In doing so, it makes known to a scuba-course applicant the inherent risks to be encountered in scuba diving and the proper safety practices that will minimize the expressed risks. This form must be dated and signed by the scuba student and the local instructor or instructional organization. This form can be orally augmented when necessary due to any particular diving conditions or circumstances, but the form itself should be relied upon unchanged and used without exception.

Another type of express (written) agreement of assumption of the risk by a scuba student is found in the release of liability form used by national certification agencies. However, various state laws can affect the validity and enforceability of these releases. These types of releases are explained in greater detail later. What is important here is that the release form also protects an instructor by containing a statement of assumption of risk by the student applicant. It is recommended that the PADI Standard Safe Diving Practices Statement of Understanding be reviewed with the applicant prior to his signing the release and Statement of Understanding forms so that, in agreeing to assume certain risks, the applicant understands them prior to signing the forms.

The language of the forms should never be changed for any reason or for any particular situation. If a question arises, an attorney should be contacted to determine a legally safe course of action. If either form cannot for any reason be signed by a student as printed, it is recommended that the student not be allowed to enter the course, or, at the *very least,* not be allowed to do *any* water training whatsoever until PADI is contacted and the situation is resolved. An instructor who does otherwise unquestionably proceeds at his own peril and may unknowingly jeopardize liability insurance coverage.

The PADI Standard Safe Diving Practices Statement of Understanding is reproduced in the "Standards and Procedures" section of the PADI *Instructor Manual.*

Two

The Legal Process

Knowing the rules is only half the process; to become truly competent, a person must also understand the manner by which the rules are applied. This fact definitely applies to law. In fact, much of the confusion and complexity that most laymen associate with legal issues stems from a lack of understanding of the process by which decisions are reached.

In section one, we presented the knowledge base needed to understand the concept of negligence. In this section we will explore the process of how the principles outlined in section one are put into practice.

The first issue addressed will be the "anatomy" of a lawsuit. In our discussion we will consider how a suit is initiated and follow the process through the various pretrial and trial phases to its conclusion.

Next, to avoid overly idealistic expectations about the

legal process, a few legal "facts of life" will be offered. This discussion will be an honest analysis of the realities of the legal process and will hopefully shed light on why many laymen often become frustrated when dealing with our legal system.

Anatomy of a Lawsuit

The formula of negligence helps to break down and categorize the relevant facts so that it can be determined if liability exists in an accident situation. However, believing a person has been wronged and proving it are two different things. The arena of proof is the courtroom, and the vehicle of proof is the lawsuit.

When an accident occurs, it is up to the injured party to begin a legal action. The injured party is the plaintiff. (One officially becomes the plaintiff when he files the necessary papers to begin a lawsuit.) The plaintiff usually hires a lawyer both to find out if a lawsuit can be brought *and* to have the lawsuit handled properly.

The lawyer must first determine whether a legal cause of action exists, whom or what to sue, and what the damages are. A *cause of action* exists where the facts alleged by the plaintiff add up to a legally recognizable right to recover. Thus, a plaintiff must show that his case is of a type that the law has traditionally allowed as a legitimate ground upon which to pursue recovery of damages. An example will help to understand when there exists a cause of action.

> A scuba diver gets into trouble on the surface. A boat operator proceeds by the panicked diver, ignoring the diver's cries for help. The diver suffers injury.

With these facts, does the diver have a cause of action against the boat operator? No. The diver cannot show any duty on the part of the boat operator to help the diver. There is no cause of action based on negligence because a necessary element, duty to act, does not exist.

Pre-Trial

Once a cause of action is determined to potentially exist, the lawsuit is officially begun with the filing of a *complaint*. A complaint is designed to give a defendant (the person being sued) sufficient notice of the nature of the case so that the defendant can respond to the complaint. The complaint states who the plaintiff (or plaintiffs) is, who the defendant (or defendants) is, the causes of action (there can be more than one) or legal theories upon which the complaint is based, some facts in support of the causes of action, and an allegation of the damages.

Upon the complaint being filed, the plaintiff must obtain *service* upon the defendant. This action requires the defendant to be properly served with a summons and a copy of the complaint by an authorized process server. The summons and copy of the complaint are usually handed to the defendant or left at his last and usual place of residence or business. The process server then fills out the summons stating how the service was accomplished. This statement is called the *return of service* and is filed with the court to assure that the defendant has proper notice of the suit. Service also grants a court *jurisdiction* over the defendant, meaning the court then has authority to hear the lawsuit and to make orders and judgments binding both parties.

Once service on the defendant is made, the defendant then has a certain period of time to file an *answer.* The answer indicates which issues are in dispute and which will require a trial. The answer basically contains the defendant's admittance or denial of each element of the plaintiff's complaint. By admitting certain of the plaintiff's allegations as true, the answer eliminates having to prove items in court that are obvious and not essential to the trial of the case. If an answer is not filed, the plaintiff's facts are taken as true and unchallenged and the plaintiff wins by *default.* Default rarely occurs in any substantial case.

Once the complaint and answer are filed, each side may take advantage of *discovery* procedures. Discovery is a general term that encompasses various procedures open to the parties by which each side discovers from the other side their version of the facts and their evidence in support of such facts. The different types of discovery are available equally to both sides. This is an important part of a case because discovery allows one side to find out the position of the other side *and* the strength or weakness of that position. Many cases are won or lost on how much or how little discovery is utilized.

One type of discovery involves *interrogatories.* Interrogatories are a set of written questions prepared by one party and sent to the opposing party to be answered under oath. The answering party has a limited amount of time to compose written answers that must be returned to the asking party. Interrogatory answers not only provide helpful information about the facts but also provide the basis for further discovery procedures (such as asking the names of possible witnesses). Additionally, interrogatories may be introduced as evidence in court.

Another procedure is called the *deposition.* Depositions are usually conducted by oral examination, though on rare occasions, they are based on written questions. A *deposition* is a procedure whereby one party, through his attorney, orally questions (or deposes) an opposing party or witness under oath and in front of a stenographer who copies down all that is said. Normally, this procedure is done in the attorney's office. The questioner is allowed broad discretion as to subject matter. The right of taking a deposition includes the power to require the answering person to bring along any requested records and documents about which the answering person may be questioned.

Depositions serve several purposes. They provide in-depth discovery of another person's version of an incident, information about other persons involved and even background or personal information that may provide leads to pertinent facts.

Depositions can also serve a useful propose by providing the attorney an opportunity to evaluate the quality of a witness. Similarly, useful information can also be determined concerning what type of an impression an individual may make on a jury.

Depositions may be taken of someone on the same side of the case to preserve that person's testimony if they are aged, very ill or plan to leave the country. The full or partial transcript of a deposition may be introduced at the trial under certain types of circumstances. One common use of a deposition being introduced at trial is to show that certain testimony stated in court is substantially different from what was said during the taking of the deposition while under oath.

Other types of discovery include production of documents where one party can demand copies of certain documents and papers from the opposing party, the right to enter land or buildings to inspect them, and the right to physical and mental examinations of a party. For the scuba instructor, such documents can include lesson plans, curricula, test results, accident reports and so on.

Therefore, the importance of properly maintaining these documents cannot be overstressed. Obviously, discovery takes a good amount of time to plan, prepare and complete.

Once both sides have finished discovery, a trial date is set by the court. A case may be tried before a jury or, if both sides agree, in front of a judge only.

The Trial

If it is a jury trial, the jury must first be selected. Twelve-member juries are traditional, but juries may be composed of less than twelve. The process of selecting the jury is called *voir dire,* which means *to see, to say.* Essentially, this is the process in which the potential jurors are questioned by the judge (or by the attorneys, depending upon the law of the particular state or federal jurisdiction) to determine their ability to be impartial (considering only the facts); whether they have any relationship with the plaintiff, defendant and witnesses; and whether they have any bias or prejudice they wish to admit.

The trial begins with the plaintiff's side presenting its side of the case first. The plaintiff's attorney gives an opening statement outlining the evidence to be presented. Then the plaintiff and any witnesses called on behalf of the plaintiff take the stand under oath and give what is called *direct testimony,* or testimony offered in support of the plaintiff's case. Documents and other evidence may be introduced in support of the case. After each witness finishes with direct testimony, they are then questioned, if desired, by the opposing attorney. This is called *cross-examination.* At the conclusion of the plaintiff's side of the case, the plaintiff rests, meaning that is the end of the plaintiff's presentation. The defendant then gives an open ing statement (if one hasn't already been given at the beginning of the trial at the defendant's option) and presents the testimony of the defendant and his witnesses, each of whom are subject to cross-examination by the plaintiff's attorney.

At the close of the defendant's presentation, each side's attorney makes a *closing argument* to the judge. The closing argument consists of a summary of the evidence that is given in a manner that is most favorable to the side giving the argument.

If there is a jury, the judge then gives the jury *instructions.* Instructions state the applicable principles of law of the case, and the jury must apply these principles to the facts it believes to be true. Juries must decide which side's version of the facts shall prevail, and they must also decide the amount of money damages to be awarded if they find for the plaintiff.

Trials can be an involved, time-consuming and demanding process for the parties and their attorneys. It's not surprising that most civil cases are settled prior to trial. The decision to settle is further affected by crowded court calendars that delay court dates for lengthy periods.

A trial is a complex process that is best left to the experts — attorneys. It may be helpful for scuba instructors to realize that PADI liability insurance coverage has historically included providing representation by an attorney at no cost to an instructor who is claimed against by a scuba student. This area will be discussed in more detail in a later section.

Some Facts of Life

Quite often, people are naive to the realities of the legal system. To many who become involved in a lawsuit by choice or chance, what was expected to be a fair, efficient and speedy process often turns out to be a lengthy, cumbersome and frustrating experience. Some of this negativity can be attributed to an unreal level of expectation.

Let's look at some realities of the legal process. Hopefully, this overview will have some impact on the teaching conduct of scuba instructors. In having a more practical understanding of such realities, instructors should develop a greater awareness of the importance of caution and foresight during instruction, rather than assuming without much thought that they are "legally right" in a certain pattern of conduct without taking appropriate steps to ensure that their instructional conduct is not only proper but defensible also.

The Appearance of Truth

The first reality we shall call the *appearance of truth.* Most people assume that if they are in the right, they shall prevail in a lawsuit. Simply stated, it doesn't always work that way. Judges and juries have no mystical powers enabling them to somehow discover the actual truth. They were not present at the time and place of the incident that caused the lawsuit and must therefore reach a verdict based only on the evidence produced in court (and which evidence is subject to restrictions by rules of evidence).

The verdict of a case is founded upon the more believable version of the two sides. Which witnesses seemed more believable, or "truthful?" Which side produced the more impressive evidence? Which side produced witnesses and evidence in a more believable and compelling manner? Which side evokes more sympathy? These are some of the considerations that determine the eventual verdict, and they often confuse the layperson because they seem to have nothing to do with truth and a just cause.

Litigation is based on the adversary process. Each side has an attorney who attempts to establish the facts most favorable to his client. Each side digs out the evidence and presents it not only in support of its own case, but to weaken the adversary's case. An attorney's obligation is not to discover "truth," but to prosecute or defend his client's case as strenuously and fairly as possible. In a sense, the process itself is ideally a search for truth, but the end result may not always live up to ideal expectations.

Given the mechanics of this system, a judge or jury will hear only the evidence presented. There is no impartial gatherer of facts, but, instead, two partisan sides presenting their own favorable evidence. The judge or jury must decide which version to accept. There is no magic involved. The judge or jury must decide one way or the other. All the judge or jury can do is assess the evidence logically and in terms of relative believability of witnesses and evidence. The side appearing more believable will win. This is the reality of the *appearance of truth.*

This reality is based on several factors that laymen find hard to accept at first glance. One factor is that witnesses, even when under oath, can be untruthful. Whether it is due to the high stakes involved, the witness' interest in the outcome or the absence of any conscience, witnesses have been known to testify falsely. Further, if a witness is confronted with a contradiction (if any can be proven), the witness normally does not break down and hysterically admit to his false testimony. This is another reality in itself. Contradictions can be a part of every witness's testimony, and such contradictions can mean nervousness or poor recollection, as opposed to untruthfulness.

Witnesses can also honestly differ in their versions of the same incident. Contrary to popular thought, eyewitness testimony is not the most reliable type of evidence. When a person is subjected to a sudden incident, the memory of the incident will be affected by bias, past experiences, emotions, passage of time and all the filters through which senses pass their mental recordings of events. Memory itself is a product of many of these things and is not merely a true and accurate recording of what actually happened.

Another factor involves the emotions and sympathies of a jury. Juries are instructed to view the evidence based only upon reason and inference. Yet, think whether a person could hear and see people testify without at least subconsciously identifying with, or being put off by, their manner and personality. The nature of the injury, the nature of the wrongdoer's conduct, the likableness or abrasiveness of a witness, or the background of a party are all examples of factors which, right or wrong, contribute to the final decision.

Cases are also affected by the mechanics of the presentations. For instance, an important witness may be incapacitated, unable to be found or unable to appear at the time of trial.

Many cases are presented wherein each side's story seems reasonable. However, people are judged not only as to what is said, but how they say it. This is a natural inclination of everyone. For example, assume one person sues another for a supposed wrong. Each person testifies, and each version sounds credible. One party, however, when testifying, stammers, speaks in a low voice, doesn't look the jury in the eye, and makes mistakes. The other witness talks in a resonant, confident voice, looks the jury in the eye, is composed and delivers testimony in a convincing manner. All other things being equal, who would we probably believe, or want to believe? Most likely we would side with the latter party, because that person is more believable and appears more truthful. This is also the appearance of truth.

Can I be sued?

A sometimes difficult part of bringing a lawsuit is whom to sue. Instructors often ask, "Can I be sued if such and such happens?" The answer is invariably *yes!* It is not relevant whether an instructor may feel in the right. An instructor may feel his part in a chain of circumstances leading to an accident does not warrant involvement in a lawsuit. But when a plaintiff plans to bring a lawsuit, it is not always clear who may ultimately be responsible, in part or in whole, for the injury. Therefore, the principle becomes a decision by the plaintiff's attorney to sue everyone in sight and untangle it later. More often than not, while it does place unnecessary and unfair hardships on some allegedly uninvolved parties, it is the only way to marshal all the facts to determine the principal parties.

An example of this would be as follows. Instructor *A* is teaching a basic class in a swimming pool. On one evening, Instructor *A* has Instructor *B* take the class because Instructor *A* can't make it. Instructor *B* brings his own assistants to the class. During a particularly difficult exercise, a student is injured. Who can be sued? Instructor *A*, Instructor *B*, assistants, the owner of the building, the manager of the building, the national certifying organization from which come the certifying standards, and possibly, the area representative of the national organization (if the certifying standards and their administration is an issue) are all potential defendants. Further, if the swimming pool itself is alleged as a substantial factor in the cause of the accident, then the designer and, perhaps, the builder of the pool may be sued

Theoretically, anyone can be sued as long as a cause of action is initially shown. It may be brought to light at some point during the lawsuit that the facts do not show liability on the part of one or more defendants, and the case as pertains to them is dismissed. But they were still sued, weren't they?

The "Deep-Pocket" Theory

There is one other factor worth mentioning, which is of practical importance — the *deep-pocket theory*. A very practical criterion of whom to sue is who has the assets to pay a judgment if the case is won. A person may have a good cause of action, legitimate injuries and a solid case, but what if the defendant is unemployed, uninsured, and has no assets? This may not seem right or particularly just, but lawsuits are largely a matter of economics.

Lawyers usually take accident cases on a contingent-fee basis, wherein they take the (very calculated) risk of handling a case with no advance fees and are paid only if the case is won by then taking a percentage of the resulting proceeds. The contingent-fee arrangement permits plaintiffs who could ordinarily not afford an attorney to obtain quality representation. But if the potential defendant would not be able to pay a substantial judgment, the contingent-fee arrangement loses its only incentive. If a defendant has no way to pay a judgment, a substantial and winnable case will not be worth pursuing. Therefore, if there are some potential defendants who have the means to satisfy a judgment and other defendants who do not, a lawyer has an obligation to the client to handle the case in a way most beneficial to the client, which means suing those defendants who can pay a judgment if the plaintiff wins. A lawyer will try to ascertain which defendants may have insurance, thus ensuring payment of a judgment if the suit is won.

A word of caution is relevant here. The deep-pocket theory is just that — a theory. Many defendants who cannot satisfy a judgment if they lose are sued. A judgment, once obtained, is enforceable for many years, and a lawsuit may be pressed anyway in the hope that a defendant's financial ability may improve in the future. In this vein, a scuba instructor may wonder if failing to have instructor-liability insurance makes the instructor less likely to be sued. Absolutely not. This would be incredibly foolish. There are many reasons for a person to be included in a lawsuit, and while ability to pay a judgment is a factor to be weighed, it is far from being the only factor, nor will it be the decisive factor.

Additionally, PADI instructor-liability insurance coverage provides the instructor legal representation and costs of suit in the event of a claim. Even if a claim is unsupportable, it will require legal representation to ensure the proper end result. Without insurance, an instructor should be forewarned that an attorney will have to be privately retained, and litigation fees for attorneys are extremely high. Defending attorneys may charge varying fees ranging from approximately $50 to $250 *per hour,* depending on the experience of the attorney. The costs of litigation can also run into thousands of dollars.

Settlements

By far, as mentioned previously, the majority of civil suits are settled prior to, or during, trial. The legal system would collapse if all lawsuits proceeded to trial. Why settle a case if it is felt that there is a good claim or defense? An answer to this question would be helped by understanding what settlement means.

Settlement is a condition in which the two sides agree to compromise the value of the case instead of having it determined by completing a trial. The defendant decides to pay an agreed sum of money in return for termination of the lawsuit and a written promise of the plaintiff, called a *release,* acknowledging payment and releasing the defendant from any further responsibility forever. The settlement is purely a financial agreement and carries with it no admission of guilt. The agreed sum of money paid is the settlement value of the case. The settlement value is a sum that ordinarily is less than the amount the parties feel may be awarded by a court if the case went to trial, but is satisfactorily based on each side's concerns and expectations.

The reasons that cases are settled are varied. There are some basic reasons, however, that apply to all cases. Settlement is largely a matter of leverage. Whether to settle and for how much are decisions based on an assessment of the strengths and weaknesses of each side's case. Attorneys are well aware of the uncertainties of going to court and leaving the final decision in the hands of what can largely be an unpredictable group of people — a jury. Often a known certainty of recovery of a lesser amount is safer than the uncertainties of the courtroom.

A plaintiff will always be forced to consider settlement in terms of court delays, which can be several years before a trial may be had. Time is always on the side of the defendant, based on the plaintiff's having to wait for any recovery and the fading memories of witnesses as time passes.

Other factors that a plaintiff must consider relevant to possible settlement are:

1. Whether the plaintiff has a difficult case to prove in terms of liability, location of witnesses, quality of evidence, and so on.
2. Whether immediate payment of a settlement amount is more desirable by a plaintiff than waiting a long time for trial.
3. The emotional and anxiety factors of litigation.

A defendant's reasons to settle may be:

1. The strength of the plaintiff's case
2. Lack of a good defense
3. Avoiding accrual of interest on the claimed amount over a period of time
4. Fear of public disclosure of facts embarrassing and injurious to the defendant's reputation or business
5. Severity and permanence of the plaintiff's injuries
6. The risk that a jury may award a higher amount of damages than expected

Settlement is usually discussed in all cases regardless of whether either side is interested. It keeps the lines of communication open, allows each side to gain some knowledge of the other side's case and sets up each side's opinion of the value of the case. Plaintiffs who feel they are right in their case and should win often wonder why their attorneys even bother to discuss settlement. However, as has been shown, the realities of law require a practical approach, and settlement is a solution to both sides in dealing with the problems all lawsuits present at one time or another.

A settlement amount may turn out to be higher or lower than what an actual jury verdict might have been. The value of a case is only an opinion, and a defendant, for whatever reasons, may agree to a settlement figure that the plaintiff feels is close to what would have been o[tained in court. As has been seen, it all depends on the factors that seem to warrant a settlement. Settlement negotiations are somewhat like a poker game, involving careful assessment of the strengths and weaknesses of each side, a determination whether the stakes are worth holding out for a trial and a decision as to the costs of pro ceeding to trial.

It is interesting to note that most liability-insurance policies reserve the right for the insurance company to settle any claim if they decide settlement is the more expedient choice. Thus, a defendant may have a good defense, but the insurer has the right to pay a settlement of the case to avoid both the costs of protracted litigation that may not be economically worth a costly defense, an the possibility of an extremely high award of damages.

Impact

The last reality to be briefly considered is the effect that a lawsuit has on the participants. This reality is often overlooked when discussing the law, but is no less important. After all, lawsuits involve people *and* principles.

A lawsuit is a complex process. The participants are subjected to an unfamiliar arena and stressful procedures The process inevitably makes unanticipated demands on parties and witnesses. There is the continuing burden of uncertainty. Lawsuits can be emotionally draining. Some participants who have not been educated to the realities of the legal process will probably be left bewildered and somewhat frustrated, especially if the process and outcome is different from their expectations. And even with favorable verdict, the process of litigation is unpleasant, a

best. It is, therefore, best to teach and conduct our programs in a manner that will minimize, to the maximum
reasonable degree, the likelihood of participant injuries
and subsequent lawsuits.

Three
Defensive Training

By now you should have a general understanding of the major legal issues relating to scuba instruction, in addition to some knowledge of the realities of the legal process. With this background, we may now begin to consider how this knowledge can best be applied to protect you as a professional scuba instructor. This section is designed to provide that protection. Consider section three the "how-to" portion of this manual — in fact, consider it perhaps the most important section of all.

In this section, we will discuss the issues of: medical eligibility, the use of release forms, how to properly screen course applicants, the implications of the use of instructional systems and standards, critical issues within classroom and water-skill training, and advanced instruction. As we saw in section two, nothing can immunize us against legal action. However, close adherence to the guidelines contained in this section will provide a considerable degree of protection should some form of legal action arise out of your teaching activities.

Exposure Areas

There are certain components of a scuba course that have particular legal significance to instructors. These components we shall refer to as *exposure areas.*

Scuba instruction creates student reliance upon the instructor, because of the instructor's expert knowledge and ability. The rating of *instructor* presumes that an individual possesses the necessary diving competence and teaching ability. Nevertheless, physical ability and expertise alone will not automatically result in safe, competent instruction. The law of negligence further requires the qualities of *caution, foresight* and *common sense* to be exercised.

An examination of exposure areas may help instructors to anticipate situations and exercise the precautions necessary to increase the safety of a scuba course. Doing so will essentially encourage a "defensive" method of instruction. Teaching defensively should not be interpreted in any negative sense. Instead, this approach emphasizes foresight, planning, caution and careful judgment. These qualities are crucial in the exposure areas of instruction in which greater potentials of legal consequence exist. If an instructor is better able to anticipate the potential risks of exposure areas, then the instructor will be better able to exercise the caution, foresight and judgment necessary to provide not only a safe course of scuba instruction, but an enjoyable one also.

Medical Eligibility

One exposure area involves the medical eligibility of a scuba-course applicant. It's important to understand that a scuba instructor is not considered a medical expert. He is not expected to make diagnoses or to render definitive opinions as to whether a course applicant is medically eligible to participate in a scuba course. This responsibility should rest entirely with a qualified, licensed physician.

Most diver-training agencies do not require every student to undergo a medical examination by a licensed physician prior to enrollment in a scuba course. Instead, the student must complete and sign a medical-history form prior to participating in any water-skill training. Only those students who indicate on this form a history of some significant medical condition are required to seek approval from a licensed physican. But, at the instructor's discretion, any student may be required to secure such approval.

Another important consideration regarding medical approval is that not all physicians are aware of certain physical and emotional factors peculiar to scuba diving. The PADI Medical Examination for Diving Eligibility form is especially helpful in this area because it alerts a physician to special-attention areas relevant to scuba diving, such as ear and sinus equalization ability and other similar concerns.

As stated earlier, it is important for an instructor not to assume responsibility for medical judgments. This is solely the physician's area of expertise, and the instructor should leave this responsibility to the physician. To do otherwise may inadvertently create instructor liability.

A physician examines a scuba-course applicant and discovers a physical condition incompatible with scuba diving. The physician refuses to recommend the applicant as medically fit for diving. However, the applicant convinces the instructor that the condition has existed a long time and has never caused adverse symptoms nor interfered with the applicant's physical activities. The applicant is permitted to take the course, but during a water-skill session, the student suffers injury due to the physical defect.

In the example, there is a serious question of instructor liability for exercising a judgment that affected the safety of a student. It may be argued that the student, being aware of his condition, understood and assumed the risks accompanying this condition. But, the student is no more a medical expert than the instructor. Further, the instructor may have been negligent in not relying upon the physician's judgment, thus possibly creating an unreasonable risk of harm for the student.

An instructor should never recommend a specific physician to a course applicant unless the instructor has exercised reasonable care in ascertaining the competence and reputation of that physician. An applicant's reliance on an instructor for a physician recommendation that results in the selection of an incompetent or careless physician can raise a legal question as to the responsibility of the instructor in selecting a physician. Generally, it is preferable for an applicant to see his own physician since that individual is probably the one most knowledgeable about the applicant's medical history.

What if an applicant is medically approved for diving but the instructor believes the student has a condition that is not suitable to diving? In this case it is completely appropriate for the instructor to make inquiry of the student and to seek further guidance from the examining physician. If the physician reaffirms the student's fitness for diving, then the physician is responsible for any adverse consequences resulting from the physician's initia medical approval.

Ultimately, the scuba instructor must make the final decision as to whom will be permitted to take a scuba course. Scuba instruction is not a right to which all persons are entitled. It is a private recreational choice on the part of both the instructor and the applicant. An instructor has absolutely no legal obligation to accept every applicant. Therefore, keeping in mind these considerations in the area of medical fitness, an instructor may exercise discretion by refusing admission to an applicant if, in the instructor's judgment, there is cause for concern.

There is another concern regarding medical eligibility that is worth mentioning. The medical-examination form should never be altered or substituted by either the instructor or the physician. If the physician has any specific concerns outside the information conveyed on the form, the physician should address these concerns in a supplemental medical report. And, unless and until the form is signed and dated by both the physician and the student, the applicant should not be allowed to participate in any water-skills portions of the course. The prescribed form authorized by the national certifying organization is a form approved not only by the certifying organization but by the liability insurance carrier also. Any changes, alterations or deviations from the prescribed procedures in properly completing the medical-examination form could possibly result in failure of liability-insurance coverage if any such changes become an issue in the context of student injury.

Releases

PADI, in addition to other certifying agencies, may require a course applicant to read and sign a release to be eligible to participate in a scuba course. If the applicant is a minor (under the age of 18), then a parent or legal guardian must sign the release on behalf of the minor.

What is a release? Does a release really protect an instructor? In what manner does a release operate? These are legitimate questions. The answers are important because a release is a legally significant document. Some instructors wonder if a release is nothing more than needless paperwork not to be taken seriously. Nothing could be further from the truth. Instructors who do not treat the handling and circumstances of the signing of a release with care could jeopardize both their legal position and their insurance protection.

It's important to understand that a release is a legal document having legal consequences. It is designed to better an instructor's legal position, but in no way should an instructor assume a release reduces or replaces the instructor's obligation of due care. The best legal protection available to an instructor is to carefully follow proper instructional standards and to exercise that degree of caution and foresight necessary to safeguard scuba students. A release should be considered a supplementary protection only, and not a substitute for the effort needed to teach a competent, safe course.

The form and substance of releases will vary with the state or other jurisdiction in which the instruction is occurring. Accordingly, it is important that the instructor has an attorney licensed to practice law in that state or jurisdiction review the form and substance of the release proposed to be used by the instructor. An instructor is not in a position to interpret when and how a release will be valid according to the laws of a particular state. This concern should be left to legal experts. The instructor is only required to obtain a properly signed release prior to the applicant participating in the scuba course. It is important for the release to be fully and accurately completed. The student's signature and date of signature should be obtained before participation in a scuba course without exception. Above all, the language of the release should not be altered, added to or changed in any way.

Courts often examine the circumstances in which a release is signed to determine whether the signer understood the contents and consequences of the release. It is suggested that the instructor not belittle the nature of the release or give students the impression that it is merely one more piece of insignificant paperwork. Instead, an instructor should inform the student that the document is a release of liability in the event of injury. He should also ask the students (or parent or legal guardian if the student is under 18 years of age) to read the release prior to signing and dating. It is up to the student to read the release. What is more important for the instructor is to bring to the student's attention the fact that this document attempts to release the instructor from liability in the event of injury. *However, under no circumstances should an instructor ever attempt to interpret or explain the legal effect or consequences of a release; doing so could result in the student misunderstanding the nature of a release.* The protection value of a release may then be lost if the student was misled about the nature of the document being signed.

A release may also contain a statement that the student will assume all risks of injury in connection with the scuba course. As we saw in section one, a person may be shown to have assumed a risk either by his conduct in encountering a known risk or by an express (written) agreement prior to the start of the activity.

To provide information about certain diving risks,

PADI has developed the Standard Safe Diving Practices Statement of Understanding. This document, which must be signed and dated by both the student and the instructor before a release is signed, informs the student of estab lished safe diving practices for skin and scuba diving. By emphasizing proper diving behavior and procedures, this form alerts a student to certain inherent risks of diving and advises the student how to minimize such risks. This form covers certain risks inherent in scuba diving, such as not being mentally and physically fit, not being familiar with dive-site conditions, diving with improperly maintained equipment, failure to follow the buddy system, failing to follow no-decompression procedures safely and properly, and failing to maintain proper buoyancy. Although this statement cannot cover all the risks attendant to scuba diving, it does highlight some of the more important ones.

It is further recommended that an instructor not overlook alerting students to basic risks that, while second nature to the instructor, may not be obvious nor entirely appreciated by the beginning diver. For instance, in northern climates, the water is cold and hastens tiredness, loss of energy and loss of mental acuity. Also, if visibility is limited, orientation may be affected and separation from a diving partner may occur. These common situations that are familiar to the instructor may be threatening to a beginning diver and should be emphasized to the students so they are understood beforehand.

One final word is that releases do not protect against injuries resulting from intentional wrongs or wanton and willful conduct. Examples of intentional wrongs are assault and battery or defamation of character. The phrase *wanton and willful conduct* means reckless acts done in disregard of the natural and probable consequences, which are generally known to result in injury to others.

Screening

Once an applicant is deemed medically fit to enroll in the course, further screening of the candidate involves a high degree of insight and subjective judgment on the part of the instructor. This involvement is especially true if in the instructor's opinion, a student appears incapable of the physical or psychological demands of scuba diving. Since an instructor is not legally obligated to accept a student applicant, there may be instances in which an instructor chooses to reject a potentially incapable applicant.

This subjective judgment may also come into play once instruction begins. For example, a student may demonstrate a continual inability to become comfortable with using scuba equipment. If this student cannot satisfactorily master a required water-skill-session exercise, objective course standards alone require the student be considered ineligible to continue. But, a subjective judgment may also be required to determine whether special attention will improve the student's skills or whether the student must be judged incapable of demonstrating sufficient scuba proficiency.

The overriding consideration in dealing with subjective judgments is to find support for such judgments whenever possible in the certification standards. Certification standards create a standard of conduct by which the instructor's actions or omissions are measured, particularly if course standards are stated in terms of *measurable performance objectives.* Be aware, however, that standards may be a source of liability if the instructor fails to adhere to them.

Conversely, careful compliance with these standards should substantially avoid liability. In this vein, an instructor should combine subjective screening judgments with observations of the student's degree of effectiveness according to certification-performance requirements. The "Standards and Procedures" section and other recommendations contained in the PADI *Instructor Manual* cover virtually every aspect in terms of judging a student's abilities, reactions and capabilities. The importance of this approach is to provide national organizational support for the instructor's judgments.

In the area of screening judgments, the existence of a methodical, consistent and sensible policy of decision making will do much to prevent any concerns from arising about the instructor's judgment process. Basing this decision-making process substantially upon certification standards allows the instructor to share this burden with the national certification agency. The instructor and the certification agency will be on solid footing regarding the basis for such screening judgments, and the instructor will have support in the event that any such screening judgment should need to be defended.

Additionally, all scuba courses are subject to certain time restraints that place a practical limit on the amount of time that can be devoted to each individual student. Subsequently, the instructor is often faced with the problem of providing personalized attention to slower students, which can inconvenience the rest of the class. Obviously, individual attention cannot be overemphasized at the expense of safety and learning for the class as a whole. However, if an instructor accepts a student whose mental or physical abilities are questionable, then that instructor must also accept the responsibility of concentrating some individual amount of time on that one student. To accept such a student and then ignore that student's possible shortcomings may create instructor liability if that student is injured.

Certification Standards

As we discussed earlier, national certification standards constitute the most significant definition of the duty of care owed by an instructor to a scuba student. The need for absolute adherence to certification standards cannot be overemphasized. If an instructor's deviation from these standards leads to student injury, liability will be clear. It does not matter that an instructor may feel that a particular standard is unnecessary or unproductive, or that the instructor in good faith substitutes his own judgment in place of a certification standard.

Conversely, we should also address the issues of "exceeding" standards. Occasionally, well-meaning instructors attempt to "supplement" training by including skills or information that are not specifically required by the course standards. While adopting such an approach can actually interfere with effective learning (particularly in system-dependent courses), it can also have negative consequences from a legal perspective. Generally, no matter how well-intended, *any* deviation from the accepted professional standard will require extensive justification and the corroboration of recognized experts, should a lawsuit arise. Therefore, the net result of a well-intended desire to exceed standards could actually hinder the instructor's defense.

Certification standards are not merely designed to minimize liability. They also provide a refuge for the instructor in cases of student injury *if* the instructor has followed those standards properly. When instructors adhere to standards, it allows the national certifying agency to back them up. Deviating from instructional standards accomplishes little but sacrifices much, since the instructor will be jeopardizing his ability to legally justify any conduct that leads to student injury.

PADI certification standards are based on considerations of student safety, student learning and prudent instructor conduct. These standards have evolved as a legally sound set of scuba-instruction principles and are a major benefit to the instructor because they constitute a substantial legal protection. PADI stands behind its teaching standards and also stands behind any of its instructors who follow PADI Standards and Procedures. It would be foolish for an instructor to jeopardize this protection by deviating from standards and inviting liability for student injury. Given the inherent risks of scuba diving, *there is absolutely no reason for an instructor to needlessly increase the risk of liability by deviating from the very standard of conduct by which he will be judged.*

Certain instructional standards form conditional agreements of coverage stated in diving-instructor liability insurance. These policies state that insurance coverage will not be provided to instructors who fail to comply with these agreements. Examples of such agreements to which an instructor must conform for insurance coverage to apply are instructor-student water-training ratios, proper signing and review of releases and medical-eligibility forms, instructor supervision of students during water training, and requiring diving equipment to be worn by students during water instruction. Consequently, deviating from certain instructional standards may result in loss of insurance coverage. These specifics are normally detailed under the "warranties" section of the liability-insur-

ance application, on the certificate of insurance and in the
actual policy.

Instructional Systems

In the previous segment we examined the value of closely
adhering to instructional standards. Yet, the question remains, what is the best means to put these standards into
effect? The answer lies in the use of instructional systems.
Unquestionably, one of the best, most reliable forms of
documentation and, indeed, one of the most effective
means of ensuring a sound instructional progression is
through the use of a professionally developed and standardized instructional system.

Issues, such as student preparedness; instructional
progression and technique; instructor qualifications; and
class organization and supervision will invariably be
called into question in the event of student injury and a
subsequent lawsuit. The standard of care against which
these issues will be measured is the anticipated actions of
a reasonably prudent person (RPP) under the same or similar circumstances. Since the members of the jury will
have no firsthand knowledge of the acceptable standards
and practices of the diving industry, they must base their
judgment on the testimony of experts in the field. If Expert *A* tells the jury that a given instructional progression
is improper and unnecessarily dangerous, the question of
whether the defendant teacher is negligent for having
used the disputed technique will depend upon which expert the jurors choose to believe. If, on the other hand, the
instructor was following a professionally standardized program, such as the PADI System of diver education, then
the propriety of the instructor's actions can easily be
established. The PADI System provides not only the re-

assurance of a professionally developed and tested curricula, but the strength of the association and its membership in support of the program and its components. Imagine how difficult it would be for Expert *B* to convince a jury that he was right and that the developers and testers of the standardized instructional system, in addition to the combined membership of the sponsoring organization, were all wrong. Clearly, a standardized instructional system that is designed and tested by a recognized, respected professional organization, which draws upon the combined talents of its own membership and outside consultants, becomes an easily identified and highly regarded standard of care.

In addition to the generalized value of establishing the standard of care, the professionally standardized instructional system can serve as an invaluable resource for the production of documentary evidence. This is especially true of the PADI System, which provides student screening forms, detailed sequential lesson plans, testing and evaluative materials, attendance rosters, written statements of understanding and consent, accident report forms and certification documents. Written documentation of this type can provide factual evidence regarding the appropriateness of the activity, the preparedness of the student, the quality and depth of the instruction, the procedures followed after an accident, and the identification of those who witnessed it. The absence of such documentary evidence, on the other hand, is frequently used by the plaintiff as a persuasive argument that the activity that resulted in his injury was unplanned, disorganized/ beyond the reasonable limitations of his experience and ability. A simple review of the preceding materials on the legal process and the responsibilities of the diving instructor should convince even the most skeptical reader that a professionally standardized instructional system is both an excellent tool in the development of safe and effective instructional programs and an invaluable resource in the conduct of a legal defense for any lawsuits that may be brought.

In addition to the general importance of a professionally standardized instructional system in the establishment of the standard of care and in the provision of sound documentary evidence, there are several specific advantages that should be considered:

Adherence to the system helps to establish the qualifications and expertise of the instructional staff — The PADI System, like most standardized instructional programs of high quality, includes criteria for the selection and certification of instructors and other people involved in the instructional process, and for the number of such people necessary to conduct a safe, effective program. Thus there remains little ground for legal argument regarding the adequacy of the instructional staff or of their right to teach. Though adhering to the system will not preclude instructor negligence, it will provide clear evidence that the program administrator is in full compliance with the best professional standards with regard to the selection of instructors. It can, therefore, assist in reducing the exposure of the hiring authority while generally guaranteeing the instructional quality of the program.

The standardized instructional system provides appropriate methods of ascertaining student readiness — In many cases, the decision concerning whether a student possesses the physical, mental or emotional prerequisites to attempt a new skill is based upon the judgment of the instructor. Consequently, when a student is injured during the course of an instructional program, it is not at all uncommon to hear questions like, "Was Mr. Wetson physically capable of withstanding the rigors of the program?" or "On what basis did you make the decision to allow Mr. Wetson to undertake such a physically vigorous instructional program?"

When the instructor's judgment on these issues can be shown to have been based on valid procedures for the assessment of student readiness and achievement, the answers to these questions can become major assets rather than critical liabilities in the defense of a lawsuit. If, as in the case of the PADI System, these procedures were developed and validated by a recognized authoritative body, then the only question with which the instructor must contend becomes, "Did you follow the recommended procedures?"

The instructional system can provide sound professional justification for the sequencing of instructional activities and for the inclusion of any given instructional component — The established curriculum and lesson format provide documentary justification for the scope and sequence of the instructional program. The standards with regard to the order and introduction of critical skills and techniques have been established and validated, and need not be argued or debated in court in the event of an injury and a subsequent lawsuit. In creating the standardized instructional system, PADI has established the professional standard of care. The activities selected for inclusion and their order of introduction are reflective of the pooled research and expertise of the best minds in the field. It would, therefore, be practically impossible for a plaintiff to successfully argue that an instructor who followed the PADI System was anything but extremely prudent in the selection and sequencing of the instructional activities.

The standardized instructional system documents and justifies the instructional techniques, the distribution of practice time, and the interrelationship between the two — Good lesson planning must include consideration of the organizational procedures, instructional techniques, demonstration and instructional aids, supervised practice, and feedback. Well written lesson plans can serve as documentary evidence of the nature and quality of the learning experience provided to the plaintiff. While, three or four years after the fact, an instructor may not recollect exactly how much time was spent demonstrating the technique or clearing a mask, or how much time was spent practicing it if he can say with confidence, "I always follow the PADI System guide to the letter," then he can easily document to the satisfaction of any reasonable jury the answers to these critical questions. Moreover, when these instructional decisions are shown to have been developed and supported by the majority element of the diving industry, the task of convincing the jury that the instructional format is safe and well-organized becomes much simpler.

The record-keeping procedures inherent in the system are essential to quality instruction and sound legal defense — Even the very best instructors occasionally become complacent about keeping records. Lesson plans become sketchy, at best. Attendance is taken/recorded sporadically. Overall test scores are recorded, but no information is maintained regarding student accomplishment of individual test elements or practice components. As indicated earlier in this text, numerous issues will be raised in the event of a lawsuit — including the order of events of the day in question, the previous accomplishments of the plaintiff and the names of witnesses who can testify regarding the circumstances of the event. Since the process of litigation normally takes several years, it is absolutely foolhardy to expect to provide the type of accurate factual information that can best convince a jury of one's instructional competence through strength of memory alone.

With a standardized instructional system, one can easily refer to complete lesson plans and extensive data-recording sources to provide the best possible instructional program in addition to the strongest possible defense if there is a lawsuit.

By now it should be clear that a standardized instructional system can be a tremendous asset to the instructor who uses it. Beyond the obvious educational values, using such a system provides a strong defense posture on a number of commonly alleged elements of negligence. It is important to understand, however, that no system — regardless of how well it may be designed — can compensate for supervisory negligence. If the instructor is not attentive to the needs of his students or is careless about maintaining proper visual contact with his class and an accident results, no system can protect him from the negligence claim that will probably ensue.

Moreover, when an instructor elects to deviate from the criteria of the instructional system or chooses, instead, to follow a personally developed curricula, he must realize that he does so at great risk. If an accident occurs under these circumstances, the instructor would be faced with having to convince a jury that his program or modification was better and safer than the recognized standard provided by the validated system or, at the least, that the alleged injury was not causally related to his personal programming efforts. In short, a nationally validated program like the PADI System becomes the legal yardstick by which program and instructor quality can be measured.

Classroom Instruction

A major component of a scuba course is classroom instruction. It is during these sessions that the instructor imparts to the student the basic knowledge and principles of diving, and how to deal with and avoid the inherent risks of scuba. A basic knowledge of diving physics and physiology, the water environment, use and care of scuba equipment, and repetitive diving are some of the important areas that must be taught with clarity for the student to translate theory into practice. A carefully planned, well-taught classroom session should maximize the student's benefits from the course. Equally as important, a properly taught classroom session is part of the duty of care owed to a student by the instructor.

The maximum legal protection available to an instructor in teaching classroom instruction is to adhere strictly to the certifying agency instructional materials (guides, textbooks, exams, etc.). Adherence is important for a number of reasons.

Precise, complete and correct use of the agency's classroom materials provides liability protection in the sense that such materials constitute a standard of conduct that, if carefully followed, is proof of proper instruction. Further, specifically concerned PADI Instructors, following PADI Standards and using the materials/procedures prescribed by the PADI System provides the instructor with a significant degree of legal protection. This protection is possible because the PADI System of diver education, and its related materials, has been developed by the world's largest diver-training association and has been proven educationally valid.

PADI quizzes and tests create documentation of student knowledge and progression of learning, and protect the instructor through his documentation that he imparted all necessary information to his students.

Student rosters and attendance sheets are important as documentation of student attendance at all instructional classroom lectures. These items are provided for instructor use and are contained in the appendix of the PADI *Instructor Manual.*

The administration of quizzes and exams are important in documenting student achievement and are therefore required by the certification standards of virtually all national training agencies. In particular, instructors should use, without alteration or deviation, the tests and exams provided by their national certifying agency. PADI makes such quizzes and exams available as part of the materials contained within the Modular Scuba Course. These exams are valuable diagnostic tools in assessing the students' understanding of the knowledge and principles of diving.

A final consideration is the importance of maintaining proper documentation of student academic progress. This type of maintenance includes attendance records and results of quizzes and exams (in addition to oral upgrades and reviews). Preservation of documentation will protect the instructor from fading recollection in the event of a claim months or years later.

Additionally, PADI insurance requires the preservation of all individual student records for at least five years as a condition of insurance coverage. Such documentation should be consistently and comprehensively maintained for every student. For documentation to be considered reliable, it must be kept routinely and maintained as an integral part of the instruction process. Maintenance and preservation of documentation will be discussed further in a latter section.

Water Training

From a liability standpoint, it is clear that the potential of risk will be greatest during water training. Generally, water training includes water-skill sessions in swimming pools or confined-water areas and open-water training dives in oceans, lakes, ponds, canals, quarries or rivers. Cautious, prudent instruction; careful adherence to certification standards; foresight and common sense should minimize exposure to liability and maximize student proficiency and enjoyment.

Liability can hinge on a number of factors inherent in water-skill training. Water training requires the utmost in planning and attention to detail. A brief discussion of certain instructor responsibilities and concerns in the context of water-skill training sessions should serve as a guide toward the limitation of legal exposure.

One of the most important issues of water training is the progression and mastery of skills. If an unproficient student is rushed through skills testing without demonstrating proficiency, a question of liability can arise if the student continues and suffers injury. This is, in fact, the primary justification for the "performance-based" approach of PADI Standards, and is why PADI General Diving Course Standards and Procedures require a student to be prohibited from continuing on to progressively more complex skills until satisfactory proficiency with subordinate skills is demonstrated. The legal importance of careful adherence to this curriculum cannot be overstated.

Instructor Supervision

Another area of concern in water-skill training is the nature and extent of instructor supervision. Any doubts of your protection in this area can be resolved by carefully adhering to the certification standards that deal with in-water supervision, such as those contained within the PADI General Diving Course Standards and Procedures portion of the "Standards and Procedures" section of the PADI *Instructor Manual.*

One very important point is that students must never be left without proper supervision at any time during any phase of confined- and, particularly, open-water instruction. PADI insurance agreements require an instructor to be in the water during all phases of open-water training. So, unless recommended otherwise, it should be the absolute practice of the instructor to be in the water at all times during open-water training activities.

PADI Standards also require the instructor to be on site and in control during any and all diving course activities. Control in this sense implies that the instructor must always be in a position of immediate supervision and be able to quickly and effectively respond to any situation.

Circumstances occasionally result in a shortage of qualified assistants during an open-water certification dive. But, this should never result in students being left unaccompanied at any time — especially at the entry level. For example, during ascent training, the instructor must accompany each student, since this is a student skill evaluation. Under no circumstances should the remaining students be left unattended, whether on the bottom or at the surface. If necessary, each student should be taken out into the water individually by the instructor rather than allowing students to remain unattended while the instructor is elsewhere.

Supervision and control must provide adequate care and safety for the scuba students. It is crucial to maintain both visual contact and sufficient proximity at all times to enable effective and rapid response in case of a problem. Training in limited visibility obviously requires closer supervision of students than in conditions where visibility enables an instructor or assistant to maintain visual contact with students at greater distances. Likewise, PADI Standards also require a reduction in the student-to-instructor ratios when conducting training in less-than-ideal conditions. In any event, instructors and assistants must maintain supervision and control sufficiently close to students at all times in order to respond to any sudden need of aid.

Supervision also requires a more strict interpretation during an entry-level scuba course than it would during an advanced scuba course. During advanced training, personal supervision of all students at all times is less feasible, such as during compass runs or search patterns. But, since an advanced scuba course involves students with some diving experience, an instructor's duty of care regarding supervision is not expected to be as comprehensive as it would be during an entry-level scuba course with inexperienced scuba students.

Regardless of the level of training, it is recommended that an instructor be in the water and in proximity to the students whenever feasible even if it is not specifically required by certification standards. In the event an instructor's conduct is ever legally challenged, the absence of the instructor from the water could leave open to question the instructor's attentiveness and care.

Finally, what about students who make dives that are not related to their training? When students independently undertake their own recreational dives at a time other than during or immediately after an open-water training session without instructor supervision, the instructor is probably not liable in the event of diver injury. An instructor should, however, strongly discourage students who are enrolled in training from diving on their own until they have satisfactorily completed entry-level certification. After such certification, if the students then desire to dive on their own prior to subsequent open-water training, the instructor should strongly suggest depth limits and environmental conditions consistent with those limits and conditions in existence during their training sessions.

Instructor Conduct

Another point worth mentioning is that the continuous conduct of an instructor during a pool session or open-water certification dive is constantly noticeable to students. Occasional lapses in judgment may result in an instructor conducting himself in a manner that contradicts what is taught to students. Leaving an unattended tank standing after teaching students the perils of this habit is a fine example. Students are impressionable, and it is foreseeable that a student, upon observing some particular conduct on the part of the instructor, may assume that it is permissible or desirable to emulate the instructor's conduct. Additionally, unprofessional conduct, such as distractions by visiting friends during a pool session, scuba gear in visibly poor condition, critical or disparaging comments about required certification standards, or imprudent dive habits, may tend to color the view of the instructor's competence. *Evidence of unprofessional instructor behavior may be admissible in a trial against the instructor in an attempt to influence the jury's view of the instructor.* It isn't difficult to foresee the adverse effect this type of evidence would have on the instructor's position.

Instructor Awareness

An instructor must quickly develop and retain a sensitivity to, and awareness of, a student's needs and behavior in the water. Understanding the initial signs of panic, discomfort or loss of control by a student is necessary to exert immediate and firm control.

For example, assume an instructor takes a student on an open-water training dive in very cold ocean water. The instructor is wearing a dry suit while the student is wearing a wet suit. The student begins to experience extreme discomfort due to becoming very cold, but does not inform the instructor of the discomfort. Assume further that they are several hundred feet offshore with no surface transportation and must swim back to shore. Does this situation imply that the instructor should also be wearing a wet suit to be more aware of the conditions to which the student is exposed? Should the instructor place an arbitrary time limit on immersion in the water in such circumstances where there are no obvious signs of student discomfort? There is no clear-cut answer, but this points out the awareness and foresight needed in dealing with a novice scuba diver who may be more susceptible to cold than the instructor — especially when combined with the presence of anxiety in the student.

Generally, the age, physical condition, observed tendencies, abilities and reactions of a student should be noted by an instructor to aid in determining the foreseeable extent of care each student may require.

Written recommendations like those contained in the PADI *Instructor Manual* are effective only to the extent the instructor consistently maintains such awareness. Failure to do so may result in instructor liability if there is student injury. For instance, assume a student who, while having mastered all required pool skills, shows increasing tension and uncertainty at the beginning of the first open-water session. An instructor who is properly aware should anticipate potential student difficulty under water. The instructor must therefore give extra attention to this student or alert a qualified assistant to watch over the student individually.

Environment

Part of an instructor's duty of care is to be aware of the hazards inherent in any water environment in which a water-skill session or open-water dive is planned. In an open-water situation, weather factors, visibility, depth, current, waves, and entry and exit areas should be carefully scrutinized prior to making an instructional dive at the proposed dive site. Any foreseeable conditions that may affect a student should be explained to the student, such as the expected depth, current or tide. Naturally, judgment must be exercised as to certain conditions that may be beyond the abilities of a beginning diver, such as high winds, strong currents, surf and other extreme conditions. Obviously, therefore, merely identifying a water-environment condition to a student does not exonerate an instructor from liability if the instructor unreasonably subjects a student to extremely severe, unreasonable water conditions that may be foreseeably beyond a novice diver's ability to cope.

An instructor should not undertake an open-water training dive in waters with unfamiliar conditions, since an instructor could be liable for a foreseeable water hazard that endangers a student by reason of the instructor exercising control over choice of the dive site and upon which choice a student must rely. A dive site that is familiar to the instructor, free of any discernible unreasonable hazards to novice divers, free of unreasonable hazards or obstructions at point of entry and has comparatively adequate visibility should be selected. The instructor should be aware of anticipated weather and tide conditions and should so inform the students.

Similar responsibilities apply to swimming pools and adjoining areas in terms of premises layout, pool depth and any premises defects that are known to the instructor to present a potential hazard. If the conduct of the instructor creates a hazard on the premises, then the instructor may be liable for the risk of harm to the students so created. Additionally, if the instructor is aware of a hazard on the premises, the instructor may owe a duty of care to warn the students or to take other reasonable precautions as part of the duty of care owed within the scuba instructor-student relationship.

Environmental conditions in open water require the instructor's prudent judgment. For instance, PADI Standards set forth student-to-intructor and student-to-assistant ratios. However, these ratios are based on favorable conditions only. PADI requires reduced ratios in the event of rough, turbid or very cold water. Other adverse conditions may also require reduced ratios in the prudent judgment of the instructor. These requirements, as well as other similar ones involving instructor prudence in the event of unfavorable environmental conditions, are important. If such requirements are not followed and imprudent instructor judgment is shown, these factors may be found to be contributive to student injury. Prudent instructor judgment in terms of instructor awareness and environmental conditions should always, when in doubt, fall on the side of caution.

Student Records

As seen in the previous section dealing with classroom instruction, a routine and comprehensive documentation of student records is an absolute must. This requirement applies equally to pool and open-water instruction. PADI provides various performance-skill forms and checklists, in addition to an emergency procedures information sheet, equipment inspection checklist, a dive roster and diving accident report form.

An instructor should develop a careful routine in maintaining student records which, if kept in a precise organized fashion, will be extremely useful in the event of legal action. PADI's Student Record form, in particular, is an excellent way to easily compile and maintain this vital information. A consistent pattern of completion of such forms tends to portray the instructor as competent, thorough and professional. Further, documentation provides evidence of proper instructor conduct in case a student's water-skill performance is questioned. Documentation may also be used as evidence of proper instructor conduct if substantial time has passed, and the instructor has little memory of the details of a particular water-skill session in which an injury occurred. However, for student records to be used this way, it must be shown that the instructor consistently and habitually maintained such records for all students as a normal part of the instruction process.

These are only a few of the responsibility areas that underlie the instructor's duty of care owed to scuba students during water-skill sessions and open-water certification dives. An instructor can properly fulfill his duty of care by carefully following applicable certification standards supplemented with careful judgment, prudence and common sense. For instance, harassing students in the water as an alleged "training technique" may be held to be imprudent if it results in student injury. Hopefully, the few general areas of concern expressed here will give an instructor pause for thought in assessing instructional conduct during water training to maximize water-training benefits to the student while simultaneously minimizing any risk of harm and exposure to liability.

Advanced Diver Instruction

Our discussion of instructor liability has concentrated on entry-level courses and the instructor's corresponding responsibilities. But as continuing diver education becomes more and more popular, the liability aspects of these advanced courses become increasingly important. Many instructors now teach progressive levels of scuba training from Advanced Open Water Diver to Assistant Instructor and a wide range of specialty courses, also. Each level of diving proficiency involves specific skills and activities each with different instructional standards and procedures.

An instructor may wonder whether the duty of care owed to advanced scuba students is different than that owed to entry-level students. Essentially, the duty of care to take reasonable precautions against injury to scuba students regardless of the level of instruction never changes. The duty of care in this regard can never be relaxed. The medical-eligibility form, statement of understanding, and the release form must all be properly reviewed, signed and dated. The standards and procedures for the particular continuing-education course must be followed precisely for the instructor to have the self-protection inherent in following the standards and procedures. As we discussed in earlier sections, instructional standards and procedures create a standard against which the instructor's conduct will be judged. If an instructor fails to follow instructional standards, and that failure results in student injury, the standards will probably be used against the instructor as a consequence. This probable consequence applies to all levels of scuba instruction.

To some degree, the concerns of assumption of risk change in the context of continuing education courses. The instructor is not dealing with a novice diver. The advanced student has acquired basic diving skills and has often gained recreational diving experience. Thus, certain assumption of risk concerns inherent in an entry-level course are less crucial in an continuing-education course. For instance, the risk of cold water affecting stamina and judgment, the risk of limited visibility affecting orientation, and the risk of dive-partner separation are lessened with an advanced open-water diver because these risks have been experienced and have, therefore, probably become obvious to, and understood by, the student.

Nevertheless, the instructor of a continuing-education course exchanges one set of assumption of risk concerns for another. As the level of instruction increases, so do the demands made upon the advanced student in terms of increased competence and abilities. Advanced instructional courses involve the risks inherent in activities, such as night diving and deep diving, and these risks must be obvious, understood and appreciated by the student. For instance, night diving contains the inherent risks of dive-partner separation, underwater-light failure, disorientation and inability to locate the proper exit site. Deep diving involves the inherent risks of nitrogen narcosis and the risk of decompression sickness if bottom time/depth levels are misjudged. Further, other specialty courses, such as wreck diving, cavern diving and ice diving, each contain their own inherent risks.

The point is that in advanced instruction courses, the inherent risks become more specialized depending upon the level of the course. PADI Standards and Procedures for each advanced level of instruction are quite detailed about the care and precaution owed by the instructor for the safety of the advanced student in terms of anticipating and guarding against the inherent risks. But, in addition to the PADI Standard Safe Diving Practices Statement of Understanding, the risks inherent in the applicable advanced scuba course should always be reviewed with the student.

Four

Special Situations and Considerations

Is there any difference in an instructor's legal exposure when he does not charge for his services? Can an instructor be held liable for the death or injury of a student *after* the student is certified? Why does an instructor *really* need liability insurance? From a legal perspective, what should an instructor do if an accident occurs? These questions exhibit only a few of the special legal issues that can arise from teaching diving.

In this section, we will deal with special areas of concern that are, unfortunately, often overlooked until a problem arises. The topics we will discuss are: Gratuitous Services and Advice; Liability After Certification; Liability Insurance; and When an Accident Happens. To be fully prepared for the legal consequences that can result from these unique situations, we should make every effort to become thoroughly familiar with this information.

Gratuitous Services and Advice

There are occasions when a scuba instructor may not charge for instruction, such as for promotional purposes or as a favor to a friend or relative. Also, Divemasters and other qualified divers who assist in instructional activities are rarely paid for their services.

In these situations, can the instructor or assistant be liable for negligence for a student injury even though there was no charge for their services? *Absolutely.* Teaching or assisting a scuba course for free does not eliminate or reduce the duty of care owed to scuba students. Once the instructor undertakes course instruction, even gratuitously, the students will justifiably rely on the instructor for their reasonable safety, and the instructor will then owe a duty to the students to use that amount of reasonable care expected of a reasonably competent instructor.

The important concern here is for an instructor to approach this aspect, in addition to all other liability aspects of scuba instruction, with the attitude that all reasonable steps should be taken not only to minimize the risk of harm (which obviously benefits the scuba student) but also to ensure maximum self-protection if there is an accident. Rather than taking a chance by assuming liability does not exist, the better approach is to ask whether everything possible has been done for self-protection — assuming that liability *may* be charged no matter how unlikely it seems. The question is not really whether an instructor can escape responsibility (which is not possible), but whether an instructor has taken all foreseeable precautions for the safety of the students, regardless of whether payment has been received.

When an instructor teaches a gratuitous scuba course, it is important that he not change, alter or eliminate any requirements or procedures that are in effect for the paid scuba course. Medical-eligibility forms and releases should be properly filled out and signed, and the PADI Safe Diving Practices Statement of Understanding should be reviewed with the student and properly signed. The course standards and procedures should be strictly followed. If a nonpaying student is injured during the course, *the issue of nonpayment will not affect the question of instructor liability.* As in a paid course, the instructor's conduct will be the focus, not whether the course was paid for.

Additionally, instructor-liability insurance provisions do not specify that a fee is required for coverage to apply. PADI insurance applies to liability for any negligent act, error or omission arising out of the rendering or failure to render professional services in the insured's capacity as an instructor. Thus, liability-insurance coverage is based on the provision of scuba-instruction services and not on whether the instructor receives any fee. Since liability-insurance coverage should cover a gratuitous instruction course, the instructor must comply with insurance requirements, such as completion of the medical eligibility, and PADI Safe Diving Practices Statement of Understanding or waiver and release forms. Potential instructor liability even in courses that are gratuitous make it crucial for an instructor to carefully follow all specified instruction requirements, standards and procedures, regardless of whether a course fee has been paid.

Another relevant concern that instructors have involves rendering advice and assistance to divers in recreational circumstances. It is not unusual during a recreational dive for an inexperienced diver, upon learning that a fellow diver is an instructor, to ask that instructor for advice, assistance or even if he could dive with the instructor. In a recreational context, this would not normally create an instructor-student relationship, and there should be no duty of care owed to the fellow diver. Practical experience has shown, however, that negligence has been alleged against a well-meaning instructor solely for his involvement as a dive buddy during a nontraining dive. Though these incidents are rare, the prudent instructor should nonetheless be aware of the potential for such actions. In trying to avoid this situation, an instructor should attempt not to undertake any services that could create a reasonable expectation by the other diver that the instructor will act to guard the other diver's safety. In these circumstances, an instructor must only refrain from negligent conduct toward other divers during the dive.

Liability After Certification

Can an instructor be held liable for a diving injury to a former scuba student when the injury occurs after certification? The answer is a qualified *yes.*

Potential instructor liability that is based on the instructor-student relationship does not end with student certification. If a student is subsequently injured while diving after completing certification and can prove that the instructor did, or did not, do something during the scuba course that proximately caused such subsequent injuries, then liability may exist. For example, a student may allege that an improper or dangerous diving practice was taught to the student (or that an essential practice or piece of knowledge was omitted from instruction) and that the student had no reason to be aware of the resultant inherent risk. If injury occurred and it was shown that the instructor's negligence directly and substantially caused the injury, this could constitute a legally acceptable cause of action.

Most often, it could be expected that the former student, in the course of gaining diving experience, would become aware, or have reason to be aware, of any missing knowledge or improper diving practice. In this case, the former student would most likely have no claim against the instructor. Also consider that, if the instructor was negligent, the chain of proximate cause was broken when the former student became aware, or had reason to be aware, of the instructor's negligent omission or misinformation.

In this type of situation, the passage of substantial time alone may protect against liability if it can be shown that the former student had gained diving experience during this time. This factor implies that it is more likely than not that the former student had sufficient time, experience and contact with other divers to have reason to have become aware of the improper diving practice.

But, while a passage of substantial time could *tend* to protect the instructor, it should not be considered an absolute bar against liability. In fact, presently, a common cause of action against scuba instructors does not involve incidents resulting directly from instructional activities, such as an accident that occurs during a training dive. Instead, many of the cases today are brought by the heirs of a diver who had long since completed a certification course. These heirs commonly allege that the death resulted from improper or inadequate instruction. Clearly, instructors must continue to be concerned with the liability issue long after a student is initially certified.

The subject of liability after certification brings up a very important point. As we shall see in a later discussion, it is most important to continue liability-insurance coverage for several years after termination of instructional activities. Doing so will protect against claims that arose during instruction but may not be made for some time. Instructor-liability insurance operates on a "claims-made" basis, meaning that insurance coverage must be in effect when a claim is made. Since the *average* limitation period in which a lawsuit must be filed is three years, insurance coverage should be maintained for at least three years. Therefore, the decision regarding how long to maintain insurance coverage after termination of instructional activities must be based upon the statute of limitations applicable to minors and adults in the particular state.

Liability Insurance

When you decide to go into business, you must also accept the expense and risk of doing business. Such is the case in all business endeavors and the sport-diving industry is no different. One of the risks of business is injury caused to others, and one of the requisite expenses of business is paying liability-insurance premiums to guard against those risks that may result from the operation of the business.

Scuba diving is a safe sport despite its inherent risks. The incidence of scuba-related injuries is relatively low. However, the potential for serious injury resulting from a scuba-instruction accident is higher as compared to some other recreational activities. Instructor-liability insurance is the best protection against this potential risk and should therefore be considered a required business expense. Additionally, maintaining professional liability protection is also required to qualify for active teaching status within the PADI association.

An instructor should not assume that, because he has

never had an instruction-related accident, insurance is not needed. Insurance is an advance protection against a potential risk. That the risk may never be realized is not the point. No matter how unlikely the occurrence of student injury may seem, the consequences will be enormously destructive to an uninsured instructor if such an injury does occur.

Liability insurance also provides a protection to the diving public. Given the risks of diving, a scuba student should have the benefit of financial protection against the risk of injury. Generally, students, divers on a charter dive or users of scuba equipment are not insured for such risks and must rely on the provider of the service or equipment for such insurance protection.

The entire insurance system is based on risk. Insurance companies take the risk that more money will be received from premiums than will be paid out for damage awards. Since insurance companies must show good profits to remain in business, this risk must be carefully calculated. The premiums charged for liability insurance are based on data concerning damage awards, settlements, the costs of defending against claims and the insurability of the person or business applying for the insurance. The greater the risk and degree of potential injury, the greater the insurance premium will be.

This rule is applicable to instructor-liability insurance. An instructor would probably not be able to afford to pay the premiums for an individual instructor-liability policy. In fact, scuba-instructor insurance is not even available on an individual basis. Instructor insurance is sold as group coverage through a national scuba-certifying agency, and each instructor buys into the blanket coverage. The buying power of a national representative of thousands of individuals creates enough leverage to provide insurance coverage to these individuals at affordable rates. The average annual premium for an instructor is extremely reasonable, given the protection it buys.

The PADI instructor-liability insurance program is a good example of the insurance-coverage benefits that are available to instructors. The substantial PADI Instructor membership and an exceptional safety record have combined to avoid significant rate increases and to provide good insurance values for the premium. Thus, a well-run program with substantial economic leverage can provide substantial protection at a comparatively small cost.

An instructor-liability insurance policy is a contract between the insurance company and the scuba instructor. The insurance company promises to provide legal counsel in the event of a claim, pay trial costs in the event of a lawsuit and to pay damages if necessary. In return, the instructor must pay the premiums due and must follow certain requirements and conditions that include the standards and procedures of the instructional course. Failing to observe any such requirement or condition of insurance coverage could result in a denial of insurance coverage in the event of a claim.

Instructor-liability insurance has historically been written on a *claims-made* basis. This factor means that the instructor must have insurance coverage in effect at the time a claim of injury is made. The injury underlying the claim may have occurred either prior to the insurance-coverage period or during the insurance-coverage period but a claim must be made during the coverage period for coverage to apply. With this type of insurance policy, the time of injury may not be crucial. It is when the claim against the instructor is made that counts in terms of having insurance coverage.

Furthermore, it is important to understand exactly

what is meant by *claim*. A claim can be an oral or written notice to the instructor or insurance company alleging responsibility of the instructor for injury to a student and claiming monetary damages. A claim can consist of a letter from a lawyer or service of legal papers showing that a lawsuit has been filed. Although the instructor is required to notify the insurance company of a student injury, this notification is not technically considered a claim. For practical purposes, however, the insurance company may consider a claim to be in effect if it is determined than an occurrence justifies further investigation.

The other common type of liability insurance is on an *occurrence* basis. An occurrence policy is the opposite of a claims-made policy. With this type of policy, insurance coverage is available only if the injury occurred when insurance coverage was in effect. For instance, if an injury occurs while insurance coverage is in effect, the insurance company must honor the coverage even if the insurance policy has not been renewed by the time a claim is made. Automobile insurance and dive-store policies are generally an occurrence-type policy.

In understanding these distinctions, it is helpful to understand that it is not unusual for a lengthy period of time to elapse between the time of injury and the time when a legal claim is finally asserted. It can be weeks, months or *years* after an injury when a claim is made.

An example of claims-made situations may help to illustrate how this type of coverage works. The example will assume that the insurance-coverage period is for one year.

A scuba instructor purchases liability insurance for two years (from January 1, 1981 to December 31, 1982). The instructor then terminates the insurance as of December 31, 1982 and becomes uninsured. Unknown to the instructor, however, a

student suffered a scuba-related injury in August 1980. A
legal claim by the injured student is made in:
a) November 1980
b) March 1981
c) October 1982
d) May 1983

In a) and d) the claim was made when there was no insurance coverage in effect, which means the instructor has
no insurance protection. In b) and c), the claim was made
while insurance coverage was in effect, which would then
obligate the insurance company to protect the instructor.
If the instructor had renewed the insurance coverage for
1983, then in d), the insurance would have been effective.
But, what if the instructor only had liability insurance for
1980? In this case, there would be insurance coverage
available only in a) when coverage was in effect. Notice
that in these various examples, it is unimportant for insurance-coverage purposes *when* the injury itself occurred.
Notice, also, that insurance coverage will apply to an injury that occurs prior to the start of insurance coverage as
long as there is coverage *at the time the claim is made.*
This stipulation is referred to as *inclusion of prior acts.*
However, in any given year, liability insurance may not
provide coverage for prior acts (meaning injuries occurring prior to the start of the coverage period) so it is important to ascertain the nature of the coverage. As explained later in this section, however, the application for
insurance requires a full and truthful disclosure by the instructor of any occurrences or incidents that might potentially have led to a claim that were known to the instructor at the time of the application. If an instructor falsely
denies such knowledge at the time of application and
coverage is approved, coverage may later be denied on a
claim for the injury of which the instructor had earlier
falsely denied knowledge.

If a claim is made within this 90 days after expiration of the policy, insurance coverage will still be available. Thus, the instructor has the benefit of an additional "grace period" of coverage even after expiration of insurance coverage. Further, PADI offers reduced rates for the continuation of insurance coverage after an instructor has ceased instruction. This continued coverage is important since all states have varying statutes of limitations allowing a claim to be made up to several years after an injury occurs.

An important requirement of liability-insurance coverage is notification. If a claim is made known to the instructor, the insurance company must be promptly notified. A PADI Instructor should notify PADI Headquarters of any claim and also forward copies of any written claim papers. PADI then notifies the insurer and will forward the papers.

Even though instructor insurance is claims-made, the instructor is also required to give notice of any occurrence of injury during instruction. In the case of PADI, the PADI Diving Accident Report Form (found in the appendix to PADI "Standards and Procedures") should be filled out and forwarded in case of any accident resulting in injury arising out of the instruction course. This form must be completed regardless of whether the instructor's conduct was involved in the accident.

A claim for injury can be made in several ways. An instructor may be orally informed that a student intends to make a claim. An instructor may receive a letter of claim from the attorney for the injured student. An instructor may be served with legal papers informing him that legal action has commenced. These various methods of claims may occur in any combination. The instructor's responsibility is to notify PADI of each and every kind of notice of claim as soon as it is received. Failure to notify PADI or the insurance company of receipt of a claim until after a lengthy period of time has passed can in certain circumstances cause a denial of coverage of the claim by the insurer. Therefore, *the importance of prompt notification of PADI as to any occurrence of injury or claim cannot be overemphasized.*

Another important aspect of liability insurance concerns the information provided by the instructor on the insurance application. This information must be truthful and accurate, especially concerning information as to whether the instructor has knowledge of any incident or occurrence that may lead to a claim against the instructor. These representations are important because they have bearing on whether the instructor qualifies for insurance coverage. For instance, falsely denying knowledge of an injury occurrence that occurred prior to the application for insurance (whether a first-time applicant or a renewal) and for which claim is later made during insurance coverage may result in coverage denial.

Further, even after the insurance is in place, material misrepresentations (false statements) made about the nature of an injury incident or the resulting claim may also cause coverage denial. Material misrepresentations can consist of falsely denying knowledge that an injury occurred or that a claim was made, or falsifying the date when the injury occurred or when the claim was made. Material misrepresentations may also consist of falsifying, hiding, omitting or changing important facts about the injury occurrence or nature of the claim. An honest mistake, whether inadvertent or due to hazy recollection, is usually not a problem because it is not made with the intent to deceive the insurance company.

Insurance policies have limits on the amount the insurance company is obligated to pay toward damages. If an award of damages is greater than the policy limit, then the instructor is personally responsible for the difference. But, instructor-liability policy limits are substantial. Normally, policies are written to provide coverage *per occurrence* (claim). There may or may not be a specified *aggregate.* The aggregate figure represents the limit the insurance company will pay for the policy period no matter how many claims are made. For policies issued containing a coverage amount per occurrence with no aggregate limitation, it means that the coverage amount will be available for each and every claim made with no overall limit. This type of policy offers the best insurance values based on the insurance-premium cost.

Instructor insurance contains specific requirements that must always be followed by an instructor as a condition of continued coverage. These requirements are called *warranties* and are listed on the insurance application in addition to being listed in the policy itself. Failing to conform to any of these warranties could cause coverage to be denied if such failure contributes to student injury.

These requirements normally consist in part of already-existing instruction standards, such as open-water student-instructor ratios, proper assistant and student supervision, proper completion and signing of medical fitness and release forms and preservation of all scuba-course paperwork for a required number of years.

There are some significant practical concerns that illustrate the absolute necessity of instructor insurance. An insurance policy not only provides coverage that pays for damage awards, it also provides for an attorney and payment of lawsuit costs. These provisions are crucially important to the instructor. Without liability insurance, an instructor must choose his attorney with no assurance of that attorney's expertise in defending a scuba-instruction negligence claim. And, attorneys charge an hourly rate that may range, depending upon the experience of the attorney, between approximately $50 per hour and $200 per hour or more. The defense of a substantial liability case will cost thousands of dollars. These economic realities are important to remember. An instructor may feel he teaches a safe, careful course and that liability insurance is unnecessary. Being in the right, however, does *not* prevent a lawsuit. Even if a claim is eventually determined groundless, it can still cost thousands of dollars to defend. Turning down one million dollars of insurance coverage merely to save a couple hundred dollars of premium costs is simply a very risky economic choice indeed.

Another practical reason to have insurance coverage stems from the length of time a judgment for damages against an instructor will be in effect. An instructor may believe that not having insurance will discourage lawsuits. However, judgments are good for many years, and an instructor's personal assets, including wages, will be subject to this judgment for a long time.

In the case of an employed instructor, the question of whether adequate coverage for the instructor and his assistants has been provided by the employer arises. Instructors and assistants may be included in a properly written policy. Nevertheless, insurance coverage is too important to be left to chance. An employee instructor should verify the employer's coverage to make sure that the instructor is included in the insurance coverage and that his instructional activities are covered.

PADI offers many types of scuba-related insurance coverage, such as general dive-store liability, instructor liability, dive-store contents, inventory and loss of income and dive-boat liability. PADI "Standards and Procedures" contain an informative liability-insurance overview, and more-detailed liability-insurance information is available from PADI.

When An Accident Happens

In trying to be prepared for a potential serious student injury during instruction, instructors should be aware of several *dos* and *don'ts.*

Naturally, an instructor should render prompt and competent rescue, first aid and transport to an appropriate facility if necessary. An instructor may offer words of comfort and concern to the injured student.

However, *under no circumstances whatsoever should the instructor speculate about how an injury happened with anyone present.* There may be an exception to this if a law-enforcement officer arrives at the scene, but any statements made should be as concise and factual as possible. It is probably not a good idea to refuse to respond to a law-enforcement official on the ground that the instructor's lawyer must first be consulted. This refusal to respond may be admitted into any potential lawsuit and may be used to depict the instructor as calculating and conniving in the face of injury to a student. Any expressions of concern spoken to the injured person or in the presence of witnesses should be limited to the well-being of the injured student. Expressions of fault as to the accident should not be spoken, since they may be interpreted as implied admission of responsibility.

The instructor should not immediately discuss the incident with any other students, instructors or assistants who were present when the injury occurred without the advice of a lawyer. These individuals may be called as witnesses, and if the rules of evidence allow, the instructor's statements, if damaging, may be admitted against the instructor. It is *not* harmful, however, for the instructor to solicit the recollections of the other students, instructors or assistants who witnessed the circumstances that led up to the injury. The instructor should not repeat these recollections to anyone other than a representative of the instructor's liability insurer or a lawyer engaged by the liability insurer.

It is recommended that the instructor note the identities of all persons present when the accident occurred, because it may be more difficult to recall such details later on.

It is entirely appropriate for the instructor to notify the family of the injured student as soon as practically possible. This call should be made even if any authorities indicate they will assume responsibility for such notification. Once again, the instructor should refrain as much as possible from discussing the circumstances of the accident and from expressing any responsibility that may later be interpreted as an admission of fault.

The instructor must also notify his certification agency as soon as possible. The agency will then provide any necessary information or guidance and will notify the liability insurer. Additionally, the instructor must notify any other general liability or homeowner insurers under which he is covered. If the accident involves motor vehicles, the instructor must notify his automobile-insurance carrier. If the accident occurs on property owned or leased by another, that owner or lessee should be notified as soon as possible. In the event the instructor is working as an employee, assistant or independent contractor of another person or organization, then that person or organization must be notified. Additionally, if the injured student was using any rented scuba equipment, then the lessor of the equipment should be notified. Once again, these notifications should be restricted to the minimum information necessary, and expressions of fault or statements about the accident should not be made.

The question of the injured student's scuba equipment should be addressed. The instructor should ensure that the equipment is collected and stored without alteration, change or disassembly until otherwise directed by a person with appropriate authority. Of course, if someone at the site of the accident has the appropriate authority to be responsible for the equipment, such as a law-enforcement officer, and requests possession of the equipment, this may be done. If a student injury is fatal, it is common for the victim's equipment to be turned over to law-enforcement authorities.

Soon after the accident, the instructor should write down in detail his recollection of events leading up to, during and immediately after the accident. This account should include any statements made by people at the scene of the accident. Further, anything unusual or relevant about the state of the injured person's scuba equipment should be noted. The existence of any such writings should be disclosed only to the liability-insurance company and its attorney, once the attorney assigned to represent the instructor (in the event of a claim) is in contact. This measure will greatly assist the investigation and potential defense in the event of a claim.

It is sincerely hoped that an instructor will never have to encounter a serious injury to a student during instruction. Nevertheless, realities require that an instructor be prepared for such eventuality. It must be emphasized that an instructor's interest in minimizing adverse legal consequences in the wake of an accident need not be viewed as unfeeling or selfish. Ultimately, the issue of fault revolves around the events leading up to the accident and the instructor's conduct involved in such events. An instructor should not take the chance of inadvertently doing anything after the accident that could lead to an ambiguous interpretation against the instructor. These suggestions of self-protection are exercised in all business activities, and, in this context, scuba instruction is no different. Further, these realistic concerns also need not be incompatible with any sincere feelings of concern, support and comfort that may need to be heard by the family of the injured student.

Five

Business and Noninstructional Matters

Of course, not all of what a diving professional does involves instruction. In fact, many professionals within the industry, such as store managers and dive-boat operators, often have no involvement in teaching whatsoever. Yet, they still have certain legal responsibilities. Is, for example, an employer responsible for the actions of an employee, if that employee violates a directive of the employer? Is a dive-store owner responsible for injury resulting from a mistake made by a manufacturer? Is a dive-store owner responsible for *any* injury that occurs on his premises? Can an employee sue an employer for a work-related injury? What responsibility does a charter-boat captain have once his passengers (divers) are in the water?

These and other similar questions should be of great concern to any member of the diving industry. As with diving instructors, other industry professionals must realize that failing to adequately understand and take appropriate action to fulfill their duties can have serious consequences.

This final section will deal with a multitude of diverse issues designed to acquaint you with possible legal implications primarily arising from noninstructional activities. The topics we will discuss are: Employer-Employee Relationships, Product Liability, Premises Liability, Workmen's Compensation, and liability in the operation of Dive-Charter Boats.

Employer-Employee Relationships

When considering employer-employee relationships, the essential legal principle to be remembered above all is that in most circumstances, the employer is legally responsible for the negligent (wrongful) conduct of the employee. This principle of law, sometimes referred to as *vicarious liability* or *respondeat superior,* charges the legal responsibility for the negligent conduct of an employee to the employer. The negligence of an employee will be charged to the employer even though the employer did not know about, or encourage, the employee's wrongful conduct. Even if an employer has taken steps to guard against the negligence of the employee, an employer will still probably be responsible for the employee's wrongful conduct.

This rule is somewhat harsh by saying that the employer can be liable even if the employer has done his best to prevent harmful employee conduct. What the law is really saying is that between an employer and an employee, the one who is in the better position to assert general control is the employer — and the employer must assume this burden of control or else bear the loss.

Also relevant to our discussion is how the employee relationship is defined, and what consequences this definition may have. Take, for example, the matter of instructional assistants. Assistants are used and relied upon by instructors throughout the scuba-instruction industry. In the context of scuba instruction, an assistant is usually considered by the law as an *employee.* And as we shall see shortly, a worker need not be employed full-time nor receive a regular weekly income to legally be considered an employee.

For an employer to be found liable for the negligent conduct of the person hired to do work, it must be shown that:

a. The hired person was an employee.

and

b. The negligent act was committed within the scope of the employee's employment.

Both of these requirements must be shown before an employer may be held liable. Now, let us briefly examine each requirement.

When is an assistant or worker an employee? If the employer has *the right to control and direct the manner in which the worker performs his work,* then the worker will legally be considered an employee. Notice the word *right.* An employer-employee relationship exists as long as the employer has the right to control the way in which the employee performs his duties, even if the employer does not exercise that right at times. The important concept to remember is that it is the power to control the details of the manner in which the employee does his work that determines the existence of employee status. If an employer has only the right to prescribe the result to be accomplished by the work and reserves no right of control over the manner and details of the performance of the work, then the hired person is an *independent contractor,* and not an employee.

There is no hard-and-fast rule in determining when a hired worker is an employee. Courts make such decisions on a case-by-case basis. There are, however, several factors that help make such a determination. Some of these factors are:

1. The existence, if any, of a contract or agreement between the hirer and hired person as to the agreed performance of the work. It must then be determined whether the employer and the employee agreed that the employer would have supervisory powers over the manner and detail in which the employee would perform the work.
2. Whether the employer actually asserted control over the means and methods that the worker used to accomplish the job (suggestive of employee status).
3. Regarding the method and times of payment, whether there were payments made at regular intervals (suggestive of employee status) or one fixed price to be paid for the work (suggestive of independent-contractor status).
4. Whether taxes are withheld from the worker's earnings (suggestive of employee status).
5. The type of work to be performed and whether this type of work is usually supervised by the employer according to the industry customs.
6. Whether the worker is engaged in a business different from the employer and has special skills needed to perform tasks for the employer (suggestive of independent-contractor status).
7. Who furnishes the premises, equipment and sup-

plies necessary to do the work.

8. The length of time the worker's employment is to last.

9. Who pays the expenses necessary for carrying out the work.

10. Who pays for any insurance that covers liability/casualty on behalf of the worker.

11. Under whose name any advertising is run.

Jim Doe owns the ABC Dive Store. Doe enters an agreement with Cindy Fixer whereby Fixer will repair the diving equipment of ABC's customers on the store premises. Fixer pays no rent for the use of the ABC premises, but she must pay for her tools and replacement parts. Doe has no experience or training in the repair of diving equipment. Doe pays Fixer for each repair job done, and the amount varies depending on the piece of equipment repaired, cost of parts and time of labor. Doe includes Fixer as an employee in the ABC Dive Store liability and casualty insurance policy, and Fixer pays her proportionate share of the insurance premium. Doe controls the work of Fixer to the extent of requiring that the equipment be promptly repaired within the time promised and that goodwill be promoted toward the ABC Dive Store. Either Doe or Fixer is free to terminate the arrangement at will. Fixer negligently repairs the valve on an ABC Dive Store customer's tank, which proximately causes injuries to the customer while using the tank on a dive. The customer sues Fixer *and* the ABC Dive Store, claiming that Fixer was an employee of the dive store, thereby making the dive store liable for its employee's negligence through the doctrine of imputed negligence.

While some of the factors in this example point toward employee status, these factors are probably insufficient to establish an employer-employee relationship. Though Fixer was included in Doe's insurance policy and worked at Doe's premises, most of the factors would indicate that the employer did not have the right to control the means and methods used by Fixer to accomplish her tasks. Fixer had special skills and expertise in an area Doe did not. Doe do not withhold taxes from Fixer's compensation, and Fixer earnings were not fixed nor regular. Doe did not reserve nor exercise any right of control as to the details, manner and means used by Fixer in repairing the equipment for the dive store. Fixer, therefore, was most likely an independent contractor, and an employer is, in most circumstances, not responsible for the wrongful conduct of an employed independent contractor.

> Susan Instructor hires Dan Divemaster as an assistant for Instructor's diving courses. Divemaster will be paid a salary for the hours he works, and taxes will be withheld from Divemaster's salary. Instructor has the right, and continually exercises the right, to control and direct every detail of the manner in which Divemaster will perform his work for Instructor. Divemaster is covered by Instructor's liability-insurance policy paid for by Instructor. Divemaster does not furnish any scuba equipment to the students and is not expected to pay any costs or expenses related to teaching the scuba courses. Instructor provides the classroom and pool premises for instruction. During an open-water certification dive, Divemaster ignores certain of his assistant responsibilities, and this action causes student injury. Prior to the accident, Instructor had emphasized the importance to Divemaster of performing the very responsibilities that Divemaster negligently failed to carry out.

In this example, Divemaster would probably be considered an employee, and Instructor would therefore be responsible for Divemaster's negligence. This would be the case even though Instructor had specially cautioned Divemaster to be careful in performing his responsibilities. The most important factor in the example is Instructor's right to control every detail of how Divemaster was to perform his job. Additionally, in this example, Instructor did continually exercise this control. Divemaster's earnings were subject to taxes being withheld, which is consistent with employee status. Instructor pays for Divemaster's liability insurance, furnishes the scuba equipment, pays all expenses and provides the teaching premises. The type of work to be performed by Divemaster is customarily subject to supervision by an instructor according to certifying-agency instructional standards. Further, Divemaster possesses no separate or expert skills different from Instructor. Most of these pertinent factors are strongly consistent with the employee status of Divemaster.

Once the status of the employee is determined, it must also be shown that the employee's negligence arose while performing the employer's business for the employer to be liable for the employee's negligence. *Scope of employment* generally means acts of an employee that further the purposes of, and are closely connected with, the employer's business interests. As in determining employee status, courts also proceed on a case-by-case basis in deciding whether the facts of a given case support a finding that a negligent act was committed while within the scope of employment. Some of the facts used in making such a determination are:

1. The time, place and purpose of the act
2. Whether the acts were authorized acts of the employee
3. Whether such an act was usually done
4. Whether an employer had reason to expect such an act would be done
5. Whether the employee's purpose in committing the act was to serve the employer

Even if an act is expressly forbidden or done in a manner prohibited by the employer, it may still fall within the scope of employment.

An employee of a dive store is under instruction by the

employer not to load a speargun with a spear or projectile while showing it to a customer. However, in an effort to sell a speargun, the employee loads and cocks the speargun while showing it to a customer. The employee carelessly points the speargun at the customer and accidently triggers it, injuring the customer.

This type of conduct has been held to be within the scope of employment. If the employee is trying in his own way to accomplish or further an authorized purpose of the employer and commits a forbidden act in doing so, it is likely that this will be found to be within the scope of employment — despite strong orders to the contrary.

Some of the more difficult decisions involve employee conduct done for the personal benefit of the employee but which conduct is usual, necessary and incidental to performing the work. Negligent acts committed while going to the bathroom, keeping warm, taking a cigarette break going for a meal or running errands for the benefit of an employer have been held to have been committed within the scope of employment.

Generally, if an employee is negligent while engaged in activities solely for his personal benefit with no purpose of the employer being served, the negligence will most likely be held to have occurred outside the scope of employment, and the employer will not be liable for the employee's negligence.

If the status of a worker is determined not to be that of an employee, then the worker is an independent contractor. In the majority of circumstances, an employer is not liable for the negligent acts of the independent contractor committed while furthering the employer's business interests. Generally, an independent contractor is responsible to the employer only for the results of the work and is not subject to the control and direction of the employer as to the manner, method and detail of the performance of the work. As was indicated earlier, courts will determine this question on a case-by-case basis. There are no cut-and-dry rules that allow an employer to reliably and predictably know whether a worker will be judged an employee or independent contractor for purposes of determining employer responsibility. Interpretations may differ from state to state. Some of the determining factors may be given differing emphasis according to the existing case law of a state. Also, these determining factors may be assigned differing degrees of importance depending upon the type of work at issue in a given case.

There are some exceptions to the general rule that employers are not liable for the wrongful acts of independent contractors. Two of these exceptions are of great relevance to scuba instructors.

An employer will be liable for an independent contractor's negligence if the contractor is a careless, reckless or incompetent worker, and the employer knew or had reason to know of the carelessness, recklessness or incompetence of the independent contractor. This principal may have relevance to a scuba instructor who uses an assistant on an independent-contractor basis. Before an instructor or dive-store owner hires an assistant or another instructor to teach a scuba class or to take students on open-water certification dives as an independent contractor, common sense requires that the competency and ability of the person be reasonably determined. Generally, the law states that if a employer knew of a contractor's deficiencies and hired the contractor anyway, then the employer would probably be liable for the contractor's wrongful conduct. Characteristics, such as age, experience, training, certification or license (where appropriate) and reputation of a contractor, are used by courts in determining whether an employer may be charged with the contractor's negligence.

One indication that an independent contractor is competent as an instructor or assistant is whether he has valid certification from a reputable certifying agency. In a very real sense, the certifying agency is vouching for the competence of the certified independent contractor. PADI stands behind its certification standards and, in effect, assumes some indirect responsibility for the competence of a PADI-certified independent contractor (or employee, as the case may be) to the benefit of the employer. PADI has certified the competence, so to speak, of any PADI Divemaster, Assistant Instructor or Instructor and will defend this position as a support to the employer.

Additionally, the employer should routinely monitor the instructional behavior of the teaching independent contractor *and* solicit occasional student feedback. If any unsatisfactory conduct becomes known, the employer has an opportunity to correct it before any harmful consequences can occur.

Further, an employer should carefully review all certifying standards and procedures to be used by the independent contractor (or employee) during instruction, and it must be completely understood that the contractor has no discretion to deviate from such standards and procedures in *any* way. Again, this utilizes the protection of the certifying agency inherent in the standards and procedures to the benefit of the employer. This practice should help reduce the liability risk of the employer.

The other relevant area of concern important to scuba-instructor independent contractors relates to the *activity* of scuba diving. If an activity creates, during its performance, an unreasonable risk of harm unless precautions are taken, or if an activity involves inherent risks requiring precautions to guard against such risks, the employer is liable if the independent contractor fails to exercise the necessary reasonable precautions and such failure then leads to injury.

Thus, an activity involving unreasonable risks of harm or inherent dangers requires that reasonable precautions be taken to guard against any foreseeable harm resulting from such unreasonable risks or inherent dangers. If these risks or dangers are known, or should be known, by the employer, then the employer bears the burden of the contractor's failure to take all reasonable precautions. This duty to guard against such unreasonable risks or inherent dangers to others has been described as nondelegable, meaning that an *employer continues to bear responsibility to insure that all reasonably necessary precautions be taken, even though this is left in the hands of an independent contractor.*

Applying these principles to scuba instruction, it is probably fair to say that the work of scuba instruction involves some unreasonable risks of harm or inherent dangers that are foreseeable and that may be guarded against by taking reasonable precautions. Further, it is fair to say that a scuba instructor would have reason to know of the usual unreasonable risks of harm or inherent dangers of scuba instruction, especially during open-water certification dives.

As a result, when an instructor, dive-store owner or other scuba-instruction organization hires an independent contractor to teach a scuba course and the employer fails to make sure the contractor takes reasonable precautions to guard against inherent dangers or unreasonable risks of harm, the employer will probably be liable for the contractor's failure to take such reasonable precautions that result in bodily injury. There is legal precedence from an actual case in which it was held that scuba diving involves inherent risks of danger against which reasonable precautions must be taken and which precautions cannot be left to the employee or independent contractor.

In summary, while a scuba employer cannot completely control the ultimate legal result of any employer-worker negligence situation, he can take steps to guard against employee/independent contractor negligence.

As we have discussed, the employee should, as a condition of employment, be validly certified by a recognized, respected national certifying agency, such as PADI. Secondly, the employer should monitor the employee's conduct at certain intervals and should solicit student feedback. Finally, the employer should take great care to ensure that the employee is familiar with, and follows without exception, the appropriate instructional standards and procedures at all times.

These precautions further aid the employer in softening the burden of liability by providing support from the national certifying agency. The fact that an employee has been validly certified for assistant or instructor status by a recognized certifying agency is proof of employee competence (assuming, of course, that the employee is following the appropriate agency standards). For instance, if an employer uses PADI instructional standards and procedures and hires a PADI-certified employee, PADI is, in effect, vouching for the competence of the employee. Thus, one of the benefits of associating with PADI is that PADI will share the legal burden to the extent that PADI helps to establish proper conduct of the employer, thus reducing the employer's instructional liability.

Product Liability

Few recreational activities depend on equipment as much as the sport of scuba diving. The very nature of the sport requires the diver to be substantially reliant upon the safe and efficient operation of his diving equipment.

A scuba course includes instruction in the theory, use, maintenance and selection of scuba equipment. Upon certification, a diver should be familiar with the use, operation and care of the many diverse pieces of equipment that are used on a dive. A count of each equipment item that could be used on a cold-water dive, for example, could total as much as 30 separate items of equipment.

Because diving is such an equipment-intensive sport, it is not surprising that there is a significant market for scuba products. The scuba industry has become quite competitive for the available recreational dollars. Many companies advertise and sell competing lines of scuba products and extol the virtues of their products through advertising and packaging. As a result, divers are in the position of having to evaluate the comparative merits and safety of each such product as the sophistication and complexity of such products increase.

What if such a product does not work properly or doesn't perform as advertised? Who is responsible for resulting injuries if a product fails to operate as expected and causes harm? What if rented scuba gear does not operate properly and causes injury? What is the responsibility of a scuba-equipment repairperson? These questions have special relevance to scuba diving, where proper equipment performance can mean the difference between an enjoyable dive and a potentially dangerous situation.

These issues are addressed by the legal principles of *product liability*. Product liability concerns the unreasonable risk of injury caused to consumers by the placing or maintaining of dangerous or hazardous products in the marketplace. Generally, product liability requires proof of some defect in a product that creates an unreasonable risk of injury and proof of which defect *causes* injury.

Product defects can result from improper design; improper selection, manufacture and assembly of product components; improper manufacture; improper testing; failure to issue appropriate warnings and instructions about the use of a product; and improper maintenance and repair of a product. Liability for such defects can be on the part of manufacturers, assemblers, designers, wholesalers, distributors, middlemen, retailers, lessors and repair people.

The law of product liability is complex, and a discussion of all of the theories of product liability is not appropriate for this section. The areas of product liability most relevant to recreational scuba instruction and sales concern retailers, repairers and renters of scuba equipment.

Retailers

Scuba retailers act as the last link in a chain that supplies scuba products to the public. A scuba product is first manufactured in one place, or components of a scuba product may be manufactured in several different places. The product may then be assembled in one place, or components of that product may be assembled in different places, and the assembled components may subsequently be assembled into the final product in yet *another* location.

Next, the product may be shipped from the manufacturer or final assembler to either a middleman, such as an area representative of a product line, or the retailer. The retailer sells the product to the consumer. Occasionally, retailers assemble components prior to sale.

Generally, manufacturers/assemblers have primary responsibility for liability if a product placed in the marketplace creates an unreasonable risk of injury to the consumer. A product may be defective, or it may have been improperly designed. The defect may not be obvious upon a casual inspection.

Sometimes a design defect will be apparent and discoverable. For instance, suppose a flotation device is manufactured with an inflation capacity of five pounds positive buoyancy. Given this factor, a dive store may be held liable for injury resulting from inadequate flotation where it is foreseeable that the flotation capacity is insufficient to keep a diver's head above water while he is on the surface. In this case, at the very least, a warning about the limited flotation capacity should be provided to the consumer.

The retailer's liability for injury caused by a defective product is limited in comparison to a manufacturer, with the exception of two specific circumstances. The retailer's liability becomes more substantial when the retailer assembles components sent by a manufacturer or when a retailer causes a product to be manufactured bearing the retailer's own name, such as private-label products. These exceptions will be discussed later.

The scuba retailer acts as a conduit to the public for manufactured scuba products. The retailer is *not* in a position to determine whether each item has been properly tested, inspected, designed with due care and is accompanied by appropriate warnings/instructions as to safe use. These burdens generally fall to the manufacturer. Unless a defect or hazard in a product is obvious, a retailer cannot be expected to be aware of a hidden hazardous defect or improper design. This is especially true in today's economy where many scuba products are shipped prepackaged and presealed. It would be an unfair burden to require a retailer to open *every* sealed package to inspect and test for defects that are not immediately obvious.

Examples of obvious defects are: a noticeable tear in a buoyancy compensator, a dent in a tank valve or a split in a regulator hose. An example of a *hidden* defect is: a regulator that works properly in the dive store, but fails to operate in depths greater than 40 feet due to a defectively manufactured or assembled valve, piston or diaphragm component.

Generally, a retailer should be able to rely on the inherent safe design and manufacture of products supplied by a reputable manufacturer whose products are known for their quality and safe operation. It is recommended that a retailer spot check occasional samples of such products and encourage customer feedback on the performance of the product. If the retailer becomes aware of a defect in a product, continues to sell the product, and the defect eventually causes injury, then the retailer may bear substantial responsibility, in addition to the manufacturer.

If a retailer receives products from a manufacturer whose product quality is unknown or questionable, it would be better for the retailer to inspect and test a representative sample of each type of that product.

The law of product liability for retailers differs from state to state, and some states may require retailers to take more responsibility in the form of inspecting and testing products than other states. A retailer would be wise to seek legal advice on the extent of this legal responsibility, since some states require retailers to inspect and test products, such as scuba equipment, which could be deemed inherently dangerous.

When a retailer carries out a routine plan of inspection and testing, it would be appropriate to maintain and preserve a log of such inspections and tests. Representative samples of scuba products could be tested by instructors employed by the dive store; and the date, circumstances of the testing and test results should be detailed in writing. If a claim is made, this type of documentation could help substantiate a dive store's legal position. It would also better enable the retailer to defend his actions by demonstrating a documented pattern of inspection and testing, thereby tending to establish due care in an effort to prevent defective products from being sold to the consumer. But, for inspections and testing to be effective, they must be conducted with thoroughness, regularity and care. The testing of any scuba products should be done under all conditions in which the products may foreseeably be used by the consumer. However, retailers should first consult an attorney before undertaking any extended inspection and testing routine in order not to unknowingly assume a greater duty of care than is normally owed by the retailer.

Earlier, it was mentioned that if one of two specific situations are shown to exist, then the retailer's legal responsibility is enlarged, and he assumes the position of a manufacturer.

One such situation occurs when a retailer assembles components sent by a manufacturer. The retailer is then responsible to use due care in the assembly. If parts different from those provided by the manufacturer are improperly substituted during assembly, or if the retailer negligently assembles the parts, and an unreasonable risk of harm is created which then causes injury, the retailer becomes primarily liable.

The other situation involves the scuba retailer who

has manufactured private-label products. In this case, the retailer then assumes a manufacturer's responsibility for the inspection and testing for hidden defects, the use of due care in the design of the product, and the obligation to provide warnings/instructions for use where appropriate to prevent injury by alerting the consumer to any known dangers resulting from the proper or improper use of the product.

An example of improper design would be: a scuba tank that is designed without a burst or safety-relief disc. It is foreseeable that such a tank may be subjected to accidental overfill or prolonged exposure to heat, which could result in injury due to the inability of the tank to safely release an extreme increase in tank pressure due to air expansion.

An example of a failure to warn or instruct would be: a small buoyancy compensator with an air bladder that may burst if used with a carbon-dioxide emergency-inflation cartridge of very high inflation capacity. Another example would be: a regulator that is not designed to safely operate in conditions of excessive cold, such as ice diving.

The following example is based on facts that occurred in an actual lawsuit. In this case, the actual manufacturer was found to be 50% comparatively negligent, and the retailer was found to be 30% comparatively negligent. The deceased diver was found to have been contributorily negligent in the amount of 15%.

> The ABC Dive Store causes life vests to be privately manufactured for itself, and the vests have up to 16 pounds positive buoyancy. And the vests use 12-gram CO_2 cartridges. The ABC Dive Store has put its private label on each vest, representing itself as the manufacturer. A purchaser of the vest (plaintiff) goes on an ocean dive in tropical waters using the vest. The plaintiff gets into trouble on the surface, swallows

water and pushes the mouthpiece of the regulator away. His dive buddy detonates the CO_2 cartridge in the plaintiff's vest, but the vest does not completely inflate. The vest does, however, inflate to the capacity of the 12-gram CO_2 cartridge. The vest barely holds the plaintiff's face out of the water and swells cause the plaintiff's head to go under water. The plaintiff is now in a state of panic. Waves carry the plaintiff against a coral reef where the dive buddy attempts to pull the plaintiff onto a ledge of the reef. The plaintiff cannot hold on, and swells pull the plaintiff back into the water. At this time, there is nearly no air in the vest, and the plaintiff sinks beneath the surface, death resulting. The vest was found to have two tears that were caused by coming into contact with the sharp coral, which allowed the CO_2 gas to escape.

It was shown that testing of the buoyancy capacity of the vest was inadequate and not done in conditions to which a user of the vest could be exposed in foreseeable emergency conditions. It was further shown that materials used in the manufacture of the vest were of insufficient and inadequate strength and durability to withstand punctures and tears when exposed to the foreseeable occasions when the vest could come in contact with a coral reef. It was also shown that at the time of manufacture of this vest, there existed stronger and more durable materials for use in such scuba vests.

If the dive store had merely sold vests under the manufacturer's label, the dive store may not have been liable to the degree demonstrated by this example. The dive store would probably have been responsible only for obvious defects.

Warranties

Another product-liability area of concern to the retailer (and to the repairer and lessor of scuba equipment) is the warranty. All scuba products offered to the recreational consumer are subject to express/implied representations (promises) of the manufacturer/retailer about the performance of such products. These representations are called warranties. An *express warranty* is an affirmative promise, which is made by a salesperson and relied on by the customer, that a product will perform properly in certain circumstances. An express warranty may be communicated orally or in writing.

> A scuba diver, intending to go on an ice dive, buys a certain regulator from a retailer in reliance on the seller's representations that this regulator will perform properly in extremely cold water. After submersion in the ice-covered water, the regulator ceases to function, and the diver is injured.

In this example, an express representation about the capacity and performance of the regulator in certain conditions was made and relied upon by the consumer as a reason for the purchase of the regulator. There is liability for personal injury caused by a defective product when that defective product is offered for sale, the defect causes the product to fail to live up to any specific representations made as to the performance of the product, the consumer relied upon the representations, and the defect caused injury.

Express warranties can consist of advertising and any statements of representation, whether written or spoken, which represent, describe or promise certain things as to the nature, description, use or performance of a scuba product. A retailer should be familiar with any representations made by a manufacturer as to the nature, use and performance of a scuba product sold by the retailer. If any product seems, by its nature or by the presence of an observable defect, to be unable to live up to any such representation, the product should be inspected and tested, if not removed from sale, and returned to the manufacturer. A retailer should also be specific and consistent with his salespeople as to what representations should be made about each particular scuba product to avoid inadvertent liability. Mere sales pitches exhorting the desirability of a product are ordinarily not a warranty.

Warranties are also implied by law as being inherent in the sale of consumer products. There are two types of implied warranties. The first is the implied warranty of *merchantability.* This warranty means that the product is reasonably suitable or fit for the ordinary use and purpose for which this type of product is sold. For instance, implied warranties promise that a regulator will provide air under water, that a scuba-mask lens will not break or collapse under the increased pressure of submersion, and that a scuba tank will safely contain the amount of compressed air rated by the manufacturer. This implied warranty of merchantability is a general warranty that states that the product will perform safely during the general types of use to which the product will forseeably be subjected.

The second type of implied warranty is more specialized. It is called the implied warranty of *fitness for a particular purpose.* This implied warranty says that if, at the time of a sale, the seller has reason to know of any particular purpose for which the consumer wants a product, the seller furnishes such a product, and the consumer relies upon the seller's expert judgment and knowledge to furnish such a suitable product, then the product is represented as being suitable for that particular purpose. Concerning the implied warranty of fitness for a particular purpose, it is important to note that this law says that the seller must merely have "reason to know" of the particular purpose of the buyer for the product. Thus, specific communication of a particular purpose is not required as long as facts and circumstances of the transaction show that knowledge of the particular purpose was understood by the seller.

> A scuba diver is allergic to the rubber used in diving masks and requests from a seller a mask that does not contain the elements usually found in rubber dive masks. The seller recommends a mask made from plastic and represents that the mask contains no rubber. Upon use, the diver suffers an allergic reaction under water and is injured. Subsequent tests show the presence of rubber in the mask.

In this example, the seller had reason to know of a particular purpose for which a product was needed. The consumer relied upon the seller's expertise and implied representation that the mask would be suitable and safe for the particular purpose for which the mask was required. As a practical matter, if the defect in the mask was not obvious and not reasonably discoverable by a casual inspection, the manufacturer would bear substantial liability. In a sense, the retailer relied upon the express warranty (if any) and implied warranty of fitness for a particular purpose of the manufacturer. But, suppose the retailer had reason to know of this defect due to similar past occurrences of allergic reactions to this supposedly allergen-free mask? This would then result in a greater degree of liability for the retailer, since the retailer would no longer be relying on the manufacturer's warranties but would be impliedly making his own representations of suitability.

Let us now consider an example of a breach of the implied warranty of merchantability.

> A scuba diver purchases a scuba tank from a dive store. The dive tank contains a fracture in the wall of the cylinder, which is observable on the outside of the tank. The dive store and the customer do not notice this defect. The scuba diver makes several dives with this tank without any problems. On the next dive, the scuba diver becomes separated from a dive partner and signals to the dive partner by striking the tank with the handle of a dive knife. The scuba tank ruptures at the site of the fracture and causes injury to the diver.

In this instance, the scuba tank was not fit for the ordinary purpose for which a scuba tank is used. Striking a scuba tank under water as a signaling device is a common and foreseeable use to which a tank may be put. Thus, a product may be subjected to a number of ordinary and foreseeable uses, and the product must perform adequately and safely when subjected to each of these foreseeable uses.

> A scuba diver purchases a scuba tank from a dive store. The diver drives a van to the beach to scuba dive. The back door of the van is jammed, and the scuba diver strikes the door several times with the valve-end of the tank to open the door. During the dive, the tank valve ceases to operate properly and causes injury to the diver.

This example illustrates a point of product-liability law when, in the event a product is subjected to an abnormal, unforeseeable or improper use or abuse, the retailer or manufacturer is not liable for injury where the improper use or abuse more than likely caused the defective operation of the product.

In summary, the essence of product-liability law regarding the required duties of careful design, inspection, testing and warnings/instructions and regarding the existence of express and implied warranties, seeks to prevent the placing into the marketplace defective of inherently dangerous products without safeguards and warnings. It should be the goal of a retail dive store to maintain a meaningful program of quality control by a documented pattern of representative inspection and testing of scuba products and by a program of comprehensive observation of scuba products to ensure that there are no observable defects in a product that could subject a scuba diver to an unreasonable risk of harm, so long as this is done on the advice of an attorney to make sure the retailer is not unknowingly assuming a greater duty of care than is normally only required of a retailer.

The scuba retailer should be concerned that his expertise is being used to ensure that scuba products selected, recommended/sold for a particular purpose are indeed suitable and fit for such a purpose. Scuba salespeople must be trained not to make representations about the nature, use or performance of a product for which it may not be suitable. The level of scuba ability of the consumer and the diving conditions to which the product may be subjected are considerations that the retailer should ascertain when furnishing a scuba product.

Repairs

The laws of negligence and warranty are applicable to the repairer of scuba equipment. This relevance is very important to the dive store that performs repairs, in addition to the individual repairperson. A repairer is liable for a repair that is negligently performed and that causes injur to the user or bystander.

Further, there is an implied warranty of good workmanship in the repair of products. The consumer may rely on the repairer to competently repair and use quality materials in the repair process.

At times, a facility may not have the proper parts on hand to complete a particular repair, or the repair may take longer than projected. However, the quality of repair should never be scarified for expedience. Even if it will cause a delay of the promised completion date, a repairer should not cut corners or use inferiror replacement parts.

A dive store that employs personnel who are expected to repair scuba equipment should use care in ascertaining that an employee is competent and qualified to do scuba repairs. One way of assuring this competence is to require any repairperson to have successfully completed the appropriate manufacturer's repair course.

These principles apply equally to the resale of used scuba equipment. The retailer must use due care in the repair/reconditioning of such equipment. If such a product is represented to be in good condition, the retailer must absolutely warn a purchaser of any known defects or known variances in the product's nature, use, performance or useful life expectancy due to the product's used state.

Finally, the retailer must also use reasonable care if he performs inspections of scuba products at the request of a consumer, such as the annual visual inspection of scuba tanks. This inspection must be done carefully, and all known problems that may exist must be searched out. The owner of the tank has the right to reasonably rely on a retailer's representations as to the state of the tank's structure. This same obligation applies to any hydrostatic testing of scuba tanks.

Incidentally, if a scuba tank or regulator is brought to a dive store for inspection/repair, it is important that there be a clear understanding with the owner of the equipment as to exactly what areas or parts of the equipment are to be inspected and repaired. For instance, a visual inspection of the inside of the scuba cylinder may not automatically include an inspection of the tank-valve assembly, despite that expectation by the equipment owner. Invoices for scuba-equipment repair should describe in detail any replacement part so that it will be documented that the replacement part used was of proper make, size and quality.

Rentals

Scuba rentals involve scuba products leased to a user. The renter is called the *lessor* and the user is called the *lessee.*

The liability principles of leased scuba equipment apply equally to scuba equipment furnished by a dive store or individual instructor for use by students in scuba instruction classes, in addition to equipment rented to the public.

Generally, a lessor has a duty to instruct or warn an unskilled lessee in the proper use of products that may be inherently dangerous. A scuba-equipment lessor can fulfill this duty by requiring that a lessee display proof of completion of a recognized course of diving instruction. However, it is additionally recommended that a lessor reserve the right where deemed necessary to inquire into a lessee's diving experience, if the lessee desires to rent an advanced or sophisticated piece of scuba equipment requiring special user competency.

The lessor must use due care in the inspection and maintenance of rental scuba equipment. The lessor is responsible for hidden defects and must undertake careful, repeated inspections to ensure that the equipment is free from hidden defects that could create unreasonable risks.

A scuba product need not be inherently dangerous for a defect to create an unreasonable risk. For instance, a lessee of scuba gear may intend to make a dive in relatively deep water that is subject to strong currents. If the lessor rents scuba fins that have not been properly maintained, the heel straps may be cracked and worn. If these straps separate in deep water among strong currents, loss of fins could result in a diver being placed in a dangerous situation. Therefore, all scuba equipment subject to rental should be inspected and maintained at reasonable intervals.

Incidentally, there are occasions when one diver lends dive gear to another or a dive store may lend a product at no charge, whether as a favor or as a "loaner" in place of equipment being repaired. In these cases of gratuitous rentals, the provider of the equipment has a duty *only* to warn the user of any defects *known* to the provider. If the user of this loaned equipment is injured due to a hidden defect unknown to the provider, there is no liability on the part of the provider.

A lessor impliedly warrants to the user that the rental product is suitable for the purpose for which it is leased. Thus, a rented regulator that suddenly stops working under water because of a hidden defect and that injures the user will be a breach of this implied warranty, and the lessor will be responsible. This warranty differs from state to state. Some states require only that the lessor use reasonable care in determining that a product is suitable for its leased purposes. Other states are more strict and hold the lessor responsible for any defective leased product that causes injury, no matter how much care the lessor used in ascertaining the suitability of the product. Dive stores and individual lessors would be wise to inquire about the laws of their particular state.

A written release of liability and assumption-of-risk form should be used in conjunction with the rental of scuba equipment, and these forms do help guard against liability, if any injury occurs as the result of such rental equipment being used. A sample rental agreement is contained in the PADI publication, *The Retail Dive Store: Management and Operations.*

Premises Liability

In the section on instructor liability, it was shown that an instructor can be liable for creating and exposing scuba students to unreasonable risks of injury. In our discussion on product liability, we discussed that liability may exist for defective scuba products that cause injury. These same principles also apply to the law of *premises liability.*

The owner or person in control of land or buildings is responsible for hazardous conditions or defects that create unreasonable risks of harm and that cause injury t people on the land or in the buildings. Premises liability i based on the formula of negligence, as explained in section one. An owner owes a duty of care to people invited onto the property to keep the premises safe from unreasonable risks of harm. If an owner permits an unreasonably harmful condition to exist, the owner has breached the duty of care. If this condition or defect causes injury, the owner is responsible for the injury.

Owners have differing degrees of responsibility depending on the reason for a visitor's presence on the prop erty. Also, premises-liability laws differ from state to state. This discussion will deal only with the responsibility of div store, pool and classroom owners, in addition to othe premises owners who invite people onto the property for scuba-business purposes. People who are invited onto the premises will be referred to as *invitees.*

Who is Responsible?

Usually, the property owner is thought to be responsible for defects in the premises. However, other people may also be liable. For instance, assume a dive store leases the premises from the owner. If the dive store remodels the premises to make them suitable for scuba sales, and the remodeling activity creates a dangerous condition, the dive store may well be liable in addition to, or instead of, the owner.

In the case of leased space, the lease agreement will usually state whether the owner, lessee or both will bear responsibility for injuries due to defects in the premises and who will be responsible to inspect the premises for defects.

As will be seen shortly, premises liability involves responsibility not only for defects in the premises that create unreasonable risks of harm, but also for acts on the premises which create dangerous conditions or consist of dangerous activities. If an employee creates a dangerous condition or carries on a dangerous activity that results in an unreasonable risk of harm, the employer (who may lease or own the premises) may be responsible if the employee's negligence is attributable to the employer.

> Kathy Smith leases premises at which she owns and operates the KS Dive Store. There is a scuba-tank filling station on the premises. An employee of KS Dive Store is filling a scuba tank and becomes distracted. The tank is overfilled, bursts and injures a customer on the premises. There is no automatic compressor shutdown device at a preset pressure level, and the tank was not in a container or enclosure.

In this example, the employee created an unreasonable risk of harm that resulted in injury, and employee negligence would be imputed to Kathy Smith. Further, Kathy Smith may have been negligent in failing to guard against this foreseeable and unreasonable risk. Precautions like an automatic compressor shut-off device or a separate or enclosed filling area could have been taken.

One more point should be mentioned. If a premises owner or lessee hires an independent contractor to do work on the premises that creates a dangerous defect, condition or activity, the owner or lessee is responsible for any negligence of the independent contractor. Though an independent contractor's negligence is not normally attributable to the employer (with the exception of certain situations pertinent to scuba, as seen in an earlier discussion), the employer is responsible for an independent contractor's negligence in an area open to invitees for business purposes.

> The ABC Dive Store is having its exterior renovated. The dive store hires a contractor to redecorate the outside walls of the store. A scaffold containing the contractor's equipment is left hanging from the roof and is not properly secured. The scaffold falls, and the falling equipment injures a customer.

The dive store is liable for the independent contractor's negligence. The dive store is liable because the premises owner or controller has a duty of care to keep the premises free from hazardous conditions and defects, and this duty always remains with the owner or controller of the property. This duty cannot be delegated to someone else.

Owners or lessors of premises on which the business of scuba is conducted, whether instruction, sales, rental or a combination of these activities, should be cautious and methodical in assuring that employees or independent contractors do not create unreasonable risks of harm in the course of their work. Since the responsibility in this situation is absolute, the owner or lessor cannot be too careful in continually seeing to it that such unreasonable risks of harm on the premises are not created.

In terms of employees' daily work activities on the employer's premises, an employer should design and enforce employee responsibilities to anticipate and prevent occurrences of dangerous conditions and dangerous activities that create unreasonable risks of harm to invitees on the premises.

Duty of Care

To keep premises free from unreasonable risks of harm to invitees, the owner must fulfill two basic requirements. The owner must guard against harm to invitees from:

a. Either hidden or unobvious dangers that are actually *known* to the owner and that create unreasonable risks of harm

b. Unobvious or hidden dangers that are *not known* to the owner but that are *reasonably discoverable* by inspection

Thus, an owner must not only protect invitees from dangers known only to the owner, but the owner must also inspect the premises for unknown dangers that are discoverable through reasonable inspections. The requirement that an owner is responsible only for hidden dangers that are reasonably discoverable is an important distinction. An owner need not rip out walls or floors or disassemble equipment to seek out every potentially dangerous condition. An inspection need only be reasonable and based on common sense, foresight, caution and anticipation. If a condition is not dangerous but has the potential to become dangerous, the owner is then put on notice.

Once a dangerous condition becomes known to the owner, circumstances will require one or more types of precautions to be taken. An owner must at the very least warn invitees of a danger. A posted sign like, *Watch your step,* which warns of an unexpected downstep or a raised threshold is an example. Other types of precautions could be: barriers to keep invitees away from dangerous conditions and repairing or removing dangerous conditions.

> The owner of a dive store has been aware for some time that a piece of floorboard is rotting and in a weakened condition, but it is not obvious. A customer on the premises trips over another rotting piece of floorboard and is injured. Both areas of rotting floorboard were installed at the same time.

In this example, the owner is at fault. The owner's duty includes inspecting the premises to find any defects reasonably discoverable. Here, the owner's awareness of a rotting floorboard put him on notice that other floorboards of the same age could also be defective. The owner's failure to inspect for such a reasonably discoverable defect, especially after having some reason to inspect, is a breach of the owner's duty to keep the premises free from defects constituting unreasonable risks of harm.

Special Circumstances

There are a number of special circumstances in which a duty of care is owed to an invitee. One such circumstance involves the accumulation of snow/ice on walks and steps. Even though such conditions are obvious to an invitee, it is still reasonably foreseeable that an invitee will proceed anyway, since the premises are held open for the invitee's use. This situation requires inspections by the owner and a duty to remove the snow and ice at reasonably frequent intervals. Whether a warning would be sufficient depends on the circumstances, but an owner would be wise not to rely merely on a warning as protection against liability. It would be better to remove any accumulation of snow and ice.

Another situation of concern involves the areas of premises to which an owner's duty of care is limited. Usually, certain parts of premises are off-limits to invitees. An owner's duty of care extends only to the areas in which customers are invited. If an invitee goes into an area that is obviously off-limits without the consent or invitation of the owner, the owner's responsibility may become lessened, depending on the law of the particular state. If, however, an invitee enters a restricted area at the invitation of the owner, the owner is then liable for any hidden defects in the restricted area that are known or reasonably discoverable by the owner.

A customer enters a dive store to purchase some scuba equipment. The owner opens a trap door on the employee's

> side of the counter and goes down the stairs to the cellar to get the items requested by the customer. The owner invites the customer along to see the items. As the customer descends, a frayed rope holding the trap door open breaks, and the trap door falls and injures the customer.

In this example, the owner extended an invitation to the invitee to enter an area that is normally restricted to customers. The owner is liable for harm caused by a hidden defect of which the owner was aware or which should have been discoverable upon reasonable inspection.

Dive stores and owners of scuba-related premises should be strict about areas in which customers are not ordinarily permitted. Generally, such areas are not as scrupulously maintained as customer areas. There is no sense in increasing exposure to risk of liability even in seemingly innocent circumstances. It is recommended that any areas not open to invitees be clearly posted as such.

Conditions and activities that could create an unreasonable risk of harm should not be conducted in an area open to invitees. For instance, a compressor fill station in a dive store should contain an enclosure for tanks being filled.

Harmful Acts of Others

Additionally, a duty also exists for the pool owner to protect invitees from the foreseeably harmful acts of other people, whether intentional acts or negligent acts. An owner obviously can't predict when and how one person may cause harm to another while on the owner's premises. Therefore, this duty comes into play only when an owner has reason to believe, or has notice of, conduct of others that may be harmful. Such notice can be based on past experience and past observations. Foreseeably harmful conduct of others can include horseplay in or around a swimming pool, or a diver landing on a swimmer. In the case of diving boards at swimming pools, more than a warning is sometimes required, such as surface floats marking off an area of the pool restricted for diving.

Pool owners should be careful during in-pool scuba instruction to prevent horseplay and ensure that any diving or jumping into the pool is done under control and in an area free of people.

Swimming Pools

Many dive stores and scuba instructors own swimming pools in which confined-water performance requirements are conducted. Pools should be of special concern to owners because certain characteristics of pools can constitute dangerous conditions.

> The owner of a dive store maintains a swimming pool on the premises for the purpose of scuba instruction. The pool has depth figures stenciled on the sides of the pool indicating the depth at various intervals from the shallow end to the deep end. The pool has no markings on the bottom, and the color of the bottom is the same shade as the water itself, thereby making it difficult to distinguish the bottom of the pool from the water. It is the first pool session for this class. A student dives headfirst into an area of the pool marked as six-foot depth. However, the water is only three feet deep at that spot, and the student is injured.

This is an example of a dangerous condition *and* a dangerous defect. The defect consists of the erroneous marking of a three-foot depth as a six-foot depth. However, the condition of the pool is also defective and inherently dangerous. The lack of bottom markings and the difficulty in distinguishing the bottom from the water constitute unreasonable risks of harm. The owner of this pool would be liable for the injuries, in addition to possibly the designer and installer of the pool.

Pools should be properly designed and maintained for the use to which they are put. This practice is especially true in the context of scuba instruction when students are wearing scuba tanks and, on occasion, weights, which tend to make students less agile when walking around the edge of the pool. The walking areas around pools should be composed of a material that is not slippery when wet. If a pool edge is slippery when wet and causes injury, this may constitute a situation that is dangerous, though not apparent. If the premises also include showers and changing areas, a carpet or other nonslip surface should be in place for the same reason. A pool should be marked with easily readable and accurate depth markings at various intervals along the sides and ends of the pool.

In summation, a pool owner must be aware of the hazards caused by pools without bottom markings and with pool sides and bottoms that are the same color as the water. These conditions don't make it easy for a person to differentiate between the pool water and the boundaries. It is surprisingly easy to swim right into the sides of a pool without realizing they are there. Additionally, rounded edges further blend into the water.

Pools should have bottom and side markings or patterns, and the color of the bottom and sides should contrast markedly with the color of the water. Sanitary conditions should be strictly observed, and pool chemicals should be routinely monitored.

Sometimes, a warning of a hazard may not satisfy the duty of care. Where it is foreseeable that an invitee's attention may be distracted or a lapse of time may cause forgetfulness after a warning has been given, or where it may be anticipated that the invitees may not be continually aware of the hazardous condition, more than a warning may be required, such as repairs or erecting barriers.

> A scuba instructor owns a swimming pool where scuba class-
> es are conducted. A piece of tile near the edge of the pool
> has cracked and loosened, creating hazardous footing. At the
> beginning of a class, the instructor warns the students of this
> hazard. Two hours later, at the end of the class, the instructor
> has the students carry their equipment to the edge of the
> pool to perform a giant-stride entry. As the class carries its
> equipment to the edge of the pool, one student, arms full of
> gear, walks to the edge of the pool while listening to the in-
> structor's directions, and slips on the defective tile, sustaining
> injury.

In this example, a warning would probably not satisfy the owner's duty of care. Here, the invitee (student) was not looking for the hazardous condition since the student's arms were full of equipment. The factors of distraction and time lapse were also present. Each of these factors was foreseeable, given the nature of a scuba instruction pool session. The owner would probably be held negligent for not repairing the defect or for not restricting access to the hazardous area by erecting barriers.

In conclusion, owners or lessors of dive stores and other scuba-related premises should be aware of the design and condition of the premises. It must be remembered that if injury is caused to an invitee by a hidden defect or condition that creates an unreasonable risk of harm, an owner's ignorance of the condition is no defense to liability, if the defect or condition should have been discovered upon a reasonable inspection. An owner or lessor must conduct frequent inspections of at least a visual nature. For instance, a foreign substance on a floor that causes a slip and fall will create liability if it is shown that the substance was present long enough to have been discovered by an inspection of the premises. If inspections are conducted infrequently, hazardous defects or conditions may remain undetected long enough to cause injury. A routine schedule of inspections should be developed, maintained, followed with reasonable frequency and regularity, and faithfully recorded.

Dive-Store Insurance

To provide its member stores with protection for legal action arising from most business-related activities except instruction, PADI provides a comprehensive business liability policy. (Instruction-related matters are covered by professional liability policies). Historically, this policy has provided at least one million dollars coverage and has further covered defense attorney fees and costs for the insured arising out of the operation of store business. This coverage includes injury and property damage related to:

    a. Premises and operation including pool- and store-business-related activities

    b. Premises medical coverage

    c. Completed operations and products including sold products, repairs, rentals and air fills

    d. Nonowned watercraft and autos

    e. Personal injury including liability, slander, advertising liability, false arrest, violation of rights, eviction and wrongful entry.

Workmen's Compensation

Workmen's compensation is a right created and enacted by state legislatures. Each state has its own compensation laws, which differ in their application and administration.

Workmen's compensation is the exclusive remedy of an employee for injuries arising out of, and in, the course of employment. With some exceptions, an employee may not sue the employer for negligence that causes injury to the employee. Instead, a worker is entitled to compensatory money only under the compensation laws. Unlike a negligence lawsuit, which allows recovery for pain and suffering and results in one awarded sum of money, workmen's compensation does not provide for pain and suffering, and moneys are paid at intervals to the injured employee. Also, unlike the negligence action, compensation is awarded regardless of whether the injuries were caused by employer or co-employee negligence.

Workmen's compensation provides for periodic payments, weekly or monthly, that consist of a substantial percentage of the injured employee's wages earned at the time of injury. Compensation laws also provide for hospital and medical expenses, rehabilitation and vocational assistance, lump-sum payments for permanent injury, and funeral and burial expenses where death results. These payments are to compensate for the employee's inability to earn, and an employee must be sufficiently incapacitated by an injury to receive compensation.

Some states have made workmen's compensation compulsory, meaning every eligible employer must obtain workmen's compensation insurance coverage or must qualify as a self-insurer. If insurance is obtained, the employer pays annual premiums to the insurance company in return for insurance coverage. It is the insurance company that makes compensation payments and not the employer. However, a self-insured employer pays compensation out of his own pocket, so to speak.

Other states allow both the employer and employee to choose whether either seeks to be bound by workmen's compensation. An employer who elects to have compensation coverage must then notify the employees by posting required notices of availability of such coverage. An employee must clearly choose between acceptance or rejection of compensation coverage. If an employee rejects compensation coverage, then the employee has the traditional right to sue the employer on the basis of negligence if the employee is injured. If the employer does not elect to be covered by workmen's compensation, then he is subject to negligence claims by insured employees.

To be eligible for workmen's compensation, a minimum number of employees per employer must exist, and this minimum number varies from state to state. Workmen's compensation statutes also provide for varying categories of exclusions from compensation coverage based on employee status. For instance, many states exclude part-time or seasonal employees from compensation coverage.

Workmen's compensation laws are administered by regulatory boards set up by the compensation law. These boards initially hear evidence and decide disputes involving payments, permanence of injuries, relation between employment and the injury, and other related areas. Such decisions are usually appealable to the courts.

When an employee suffers a work-related injury, the employer fills out a notice-of-injury form, which consists of time, date, place and circumstances of injury, identification of the injured employee and a description of the injuries. Most states have minimum waiting periods of several days, which must pass before compensation benefits may begin. If an employee is still unable to work and earn after the waiting period, then benefits may be sought. If an employee is injured, but suffers no disability that prevents a continuation of work, the employee may only receive hospital and medical payments.

If a worker is totally disabled, the worker receives

periodic payments consisting of a percentage of his wages which is set by statute. There usually exists a maximum limit that, when reached, ends such benefits. If a worker is only partially disabled and can do some work, compensation will make up the difference between the total disability payment amount and what the worker is earning while partially disabled. These partial disability payments can also be subject to a maximum aggregate limitation.

If a permanent and total disability results, a worker may be eligible for total-disability payments for the duration of such a disability. Additionally, a permanent handicap or loss may warrant the payment of a fixed lump sum to the employee. Generally, compensation statutes list the amount to be awarded for a particular loss. Handicaps or losses include hearing or vision impairment or loss, loss of an arm or leg, disfigurement, loss or impairment of bodily functions or senses, certain permanent illnesses, and death.

Many compensation statutes also provide payments to dependents of the worker, such as the spouse/children, while the worker is disabled. Also, some compensation laws provide for payment of any remaining balance of compensation benefits to a worker's dependents if the worker dies as a result of the work-related injury or illness.

Until recently, the spouse or children could not sue the employer for loss of consortium, companionship and support as a result of a negligently caused injury to the worker. However, some states have begun to allow these claims that now enable a spouse to sue a negligent employer for loss of the injured spouse's consortium (meaning companionship and other inherent benefits of a marital relationship between two uninjured spouses).

Independent contractors are not covered employees

under workers' compensation acts. An employer must have the right to control every detail of the performance of work by a worker for that worker to be considered an employee and not an independent contractor under workers' compensation laws. Some of the factors used to make such a determination are the method of payment of wages, the supplier of equipment, right of the employer to discharge the worker at will and the existence of a contract of hire.

Workmen's compensation does not require finding employer fault for benefits to be paid. An injury may result from an accident, mistake or act of nature, but as long as the injury arose out of the course of employment, it is compensable.

One area subject to continual interpretation is whether the conduct of an employee, at the time of injury, was within the course of employment. Decisions in these areas tend to favor the employee.

Compensation applies to injuries sustained on the employer's premises or in areas about the premises where the employee's work requires his presence. Courts have extended this to include coffee and cigarette breaks, bathroom visits and lunch breaks, if they occur on the employer's premises in areas where employees usually gather for such purposes. Courts have also applied compensation where a worker is injured while attending to personal comfort during the course of employment, such as opening a window for ventilation, getting out of the rain or seeking warmth from the cold.

Depending upon the circumstances, injuries suffered during the course of employment as a result of horseplay or slight deviations from work have also been found compensable.

Generally, compensation does not cover the employee's travel between home and work where the employee has fixed hours and a fixed place of work. However, if an employee sets his own hours or has no one particular place of employment, compensation may cover injuries in transit. Further, if an employee leaves the work premises at the direction of the employer to perform a special errand necessitated by the employment, compensation may apply to injuries during the travel.

Employment can necessitate business trips, and compensation will cover injuries occurring during the pursuit of business on such trips. Additionally, compensation will apply to injuries sustained on the premises of, or during travel to or from, lodging and eating establishments while on such a trip, as long as the lodging or eating place is not so far away from the area of business concern that it indicates more of a personal purpose for going to such an establishment. Such trips can be required as part of the condition and nature of employment, such as sales meetings, conferences or seminars related to the employment. Generally, deviations from the business trip for personal reasons are not covered by workmen's compensation unless such deviations are minimal.

Any illness or injury proximately resulting and arising from the course of employment is also compensable. This includes a preexisting injury or illness that is aggravated or worsened during work performance.

Once workmen's compensation is in effect, the compensation insurer controls the application of the benefits and the decision whether to dispute the eligibility of a claimant. The employer needs only to cooperate with the insurer by supplying the required information upon notice of an injury. However, since application of workmen's compensation statutes differ from state to state, an employer in the scuba-diving field should consult a lawyer to determine what elections, rights and obligations are appropriate under a particular workmen's compensation statute.

Dive-Charter Boats

Dive-boat charters are common and widespread throughout the scuba industry. In essence, a dive-boat charter results when a diver, for a fee, is transported to and from a dive site. Depending upon the charter agreement, divers may bring their own diving equipment or they may have it supplied to them by the charter. Furnishing this transportation for a fee creates a legal relationship between the charter-boat owner (including employees) and the passengers. This relationship gives rise to a duty of the charter-boat owner to protect the passengers. This responsibility is the same wherever it occurs in the United States, whether in oceans, lakes or rivers.

It's important for charter-boat operators to know what responsibilities the law expects from them toward their passengers. With this knowledge, a charter-boat operator would hopefully be better informed as to what risks must be guarded against.

Common and Private Carriers

A vehicle that contracts to transport passengers to a destination is legally defined as a *carrier*. A dive-charter boat is legally a carrier. There are two types of carriers — *common* and *private*. It is important to understand the difference between the two types of carriers, because the amount of care owed to the passengers differs between private and common-carrier operators.

A charter boat is a common carrier when it represents to the public at large that it will transport anyone who desires such services. In the case of a dive charter, the offer of transport to any member of the public who is a certified diver would define that charter as a common carrier. (This would be true for any comparable transport in the same circumstances. For instance, a ski lift has been held to be a common carrier). Typical common-carrier dive charters are offered by dive stores to all certified members of the diving public.

Different circumstances may result in a dive charter being a private carrier. This circumstance occurs when the carrier restricts its transport to particular people in particular instances. For example, dive-charter boats are private carriers when transport is limited to members of a particular dive club. Another common example of private carriers are dive boats that contract with resort hotels to provide transport to and from dive sites only for hotel guests.

The carrier-passenger relationship is based on the agreement by the carrier to provide safe transportation in exchange for a fee. However, the carrier is still obligated to provide safe transport to gratuitous or "free" passengers. A charter-boat operator should not assume that the obligation to provide safe transport may be relaxed because passengers have not paid for the transport. A gratuitous passenger or a guest in a private boat would most likely involve private carriers, and an ordinary duty of reasonable care would still be owed to the passenger.

Whether a dive-boat charter is a common or a private carrier in a particular instance will determine how much care is owed to provide for the safety of the passengers.

We have seen that, generally, the duty of care requires the exercise of reasonable precautions. However, common carriers owe more than a reasonable duty of care. Common carriers must provide the highest degree of care, vigilance, precaution and foresight reasonably possible under the circumstances. A common carrier must exercise skill, care and foresight for the passengers' safety as would an exceedingly competent, careful and cautious person in the same circumstances. This is a strict, but not absolute, duty of care. While the responsibility is substantial, it does not require a guarantee of safety. There must be some reason to anticipate a risk in order for the carrier to be held to have foreseen such a risk.

> A dive-charter boat, which advertises diving charters to the public, proceeds out of a harbor with its diver passengers. The boat passes under a bridge from which some youths throw rocks at the boat. A passenger is struck by a rock and severely injured.

Is the owner/operator of the charter responsible for the passenger injury? This answer depends on whether the operator had reason to anticipate this risk. If the operator was aware that youths were known to throw rocks at boats, then, given the high degree of care owed by the charterer to its passengers, the charter boat would probably be liable. If the charter-boat owner/operator had no prior knowledge or reason to be aware of any rock throwing, then there would probably be no liability.

What precautions would be appropriate for a common or private charter in the rock-throwing incident, assuming there was sufficient reason to anticipate this risk? In the case of a private carrier, would a warning to the passengers be enough to constitute the taking of a reasonable precaution? Or would the charter boat also have to provide some physical shelter to protect the passenger? It depends on what a court would find reasonable in the circumstances. In the case of a common-carrier charter boat, however, the high degree of care owed for the safety and protection of its passengers would most likely require not just a warning but also the provision of physical shelter from the falling rocks.

So what does all this mean to a charter-boat owner/operator? In any given circumstances, it cannot be predicted whether certain precautions must be taken and whether any such precautions will be sufficient. Therefore, it is best to try to be aware of all foreseeable risks and to take the strongest precautions within reason to protect passengers against such risks, regardless whether a charter may be private or common. Remember that the safety of the passengers is the primary responsibility of the charter.

Let's go over some examples of possible dangers and examine a carrier's obligation to protect passengers. Keep in mind that a common carrier must guard against reasonable risks of harm *as well as* unreasonable risks.

> A common-carrier dive-charter boat prepares to cast off with its passengers. A passenger is inadvertently standing on a coil of line attached to the pier. As the boat pulls out, the passenger becomes entangled in the line and is pulled off the boat.

In the case of a common carrier, this has been held to be negligent conduct of the boat operator. Even if this accident was the result of only a momentary or slight inattentiveness, this incident would still be considered a failure to guard against a reasonable risk. It is possible that a private dive charter would not be liable if this was decided to be a reasonable risk. However, the amount of precautions taken should not depend on whether a carrier may be private or common in any given circumstance or whether a foreseeable risk may be reasonable or unreasonable. A charter-boat owner/operator is not in a position to make such legal predictions. The point of learning about the obligations of charter boats is to become aware of the responsibilities to passengers and to take all precautions reasonably possible. This should include guarding against all possible risks, whether reasonable or unreasonable. Vigilance and alertness is a small price to pay for the safety of the passengers and for the continuing good reputation of a dive-charter boat.

> A common-carrier dive charter takes its diver passengers to a dive site in a tropical area. It is known to the boat operator that the sun will be strong all day. The boat does not have any overhead shelter nor is there any protective sunburn lotion aboard. Most of the passengers have just arrived in the tropics and have not yet acquired tans. The trip takes several hours, and one passenger is badly burned by continual exposure to the sun. Prior to this trip, the passengers were not warned of the hazards of overexposure to the sun without protective lotion.

The risk of serious sunburn has been held to have been foreseeable, given the appropriate circumstances of extended exposure to a strong sun. Common-carrier charter-boat operators have been held responsible for the foreseeable environmental conditions and have been required to guard against the risks to passenagers of such conditions. The precautions to take are fairly simple and consist of warning the passengers prior to the trip and providing shelter and protective lotions or creams on board. The key here is to be aware of such a risk ahead of time and take all reasonable precautions to prevent any risk from becoming a reality. Obviously, it is better to maintain constant vigilance and foresight to ensure that no risks ever materialize, than to take only minimal precautions and risk liability.

Guarding against all possible dangers within a charter-boat owner/operator's experience may depend on the geographical area, type of boat and other variables. However, most risks are common to all charter boats, and some substantial attention should be paid to the scope of these risks to be aware of the appropriate precautions that may be necessary.

One area of risk, as has already been seen, may be found in weather conditions. If adverse conditions, such as severe cold or heavy waves, are foreseeable, then at least the precaution of warning the passengers in advance should be taken, in addition to other precautions.

> A common-carrier dive charter heads out into the ocean with its diver passengers. The operator is aware that a storm is forecast, which may result in high winds and large waves. The passengers have not been informed of this information. The boat suddenly encounters the storm. The scuba tanks are not secured, and, upon encountering a large wave, a scuba tank is hurled against a passenger.

In this example, negligent conduct exists. A passenger was injured because the operator failed to take precautions against the dangers, including failing to warn the passengers and failing to secure equipment. It should be anticipated that unsecured heavy diving equipment may pose a hazard to passengers during the pitching of the boat in storm conditions.

It may be helpful to briefly point out several additional situations in which caution by a charter boat should be emphasized. Care should be exercised when certain passengers are aboard whose conduct is known to the operator of the charter boat to be unruly or boisterous. Horseplay that results in passenger injury may create liability, if the operator had advance reason to know that certain passengers tended to be unruly.

Keeping a proper, alert lookout at all times is absolutely essential. This watchfulness includes anticipating and guarding against the wrongful acts of other boats. In the case of common carriers, even the slightest inattentiveness that results in passenger harm has been held to be negligent conduct.

A charter-boat owner/operator must keep the boat, its components and accessories in good working order. Also, the better machinery and appliances in general use should be employed. This practice does not mean that every safety device ever invented must be used. But, failure to upgrade equipment and to provide necessary safety devices and measures that may be called for could result in liability, if harm results from any of these failures.

Passengers should be assisted, or at least watched, as they board. The pier, dock or other such area from which passengers enter and depart the boat should be maintained and periodically inspected.

Any unexpected or sudden maneuvering of a boat should not be done without warning the passengers first. While sudden emergency may not permit time for a warning, the occasional need for sudden maneuvering is not unknown to boat operators. Reasonable caution should therefore suggest that passengers remain seated while the boat is in motion, that all equipment be stowed and secured and that handholds be readily available. However, there should be no liability if sudden stops or turns are a reasonable response to an unanticipated emergency.

Responsibility for Divers in the Water

Does a diving charter's responsibility extend to its diver-passenger once the dive site is reached and the divers are in the water? To the extent that the charter-boat operator chooses the dive site and may have knowledge of potentially hazardous conditions, such as strong currents or dangerous marine life, present at the dive site, there is probably a duty to warn the passengers of these hazards. But, once the passengers leave the boat to dive, the common carrier is normally considered to have fulfilled his duty to use extreme care to safely transport the passengers, until the passengers return to the boat.

Certain questions remain, however. Is the charter-boat operator responsible to ascertain whether the diver-passengers have sufficient diving experience to safely dive, depending upon the conditions to be encountered? Do the passengers have the right to rely upon the charter-boat operator to keep a careful lookout for divers in distress, to provide proper rescue and emergency equipment, and to undertake competent rescue measures?

While these questions have yet to be answered definitively, there is certainly reason for the boat operator to take a cautious approach concerning his responsibility for divers in the water. Particularly, if the nature of the charter agreement, or representations or conduct on the part of the charter-boat owner or employees, or the circumstances of the charter create a reasonable expectation by the passengers that they may rely on the charter boat for rescue, then the charter boat may be liable for diver injury caused by the failure of the charter boat to maintain a proper lookout or to manage a competent rescue effort.

There is no question that once the charter-boat employees undertake a rescue, it must be done properly and competently. If the rescue is performed negligently and is the cause of injury to a diver, then the charter boat is liable. Charter-boat employees should, therefore, be trained in diver rescue and cardiopulmonary resuscitation. Appropriate equipment, such as a rescue board or chase boat, first-aid kit and oxygen, should be in useable condition and readily available for emergency use by rescuers.

As discussed earlier, if the charter provides diving equipment to the passengers, then the charter is responsible for the condition of the equipment during the dive.

There are a number of precautions that a diving-charter operation can take to minimize the risk of liability and to assure a safe, enjoyable dive charter.

A diver-passenger should not be allowed passage without proof of having been certified as at least an entry-level scuba diver. Inquiry should be made of any prospective diver as to any physical problems that may create a risk of harm to that diver.

The passengers should be reminded of basic safety procedures, such as the diver buddy system, maximum safe depths during the dive and emergency procedures. Passengers should be instructed to return with sufficient reserve air in their tanks.

Charter-boat employees should check the straps and placement of the equipment of each passenger, in addition to pressure-gauge readings just prior to the dive, or in the alternative, have each passenger do this with his dive partner.

If any particular or unusual underwater conditions or terrain are known to the charter-boat employees, they must be disclosed to the passengers. Some care and judgment must be exercised by the charter-boat owner/operator as to whether the conditions of any dive site will be appropriate for any passengers who may be inexperienced divers. Additional guidelines on supervisory procedures for boat diving activities may be obtained from the PADI *Divemaster Manual*.

As has been seen, it is virtually impossible to predict whether liability will be found in any particular incident involving injury. Therefore, a charter-boat operator should use great care for the safety of the passengers whether on the boat or in the water and should take all reasonable precautions against any risks that can be foreseen. One precaution for the benefit of the charter-boat owner/operator (as well as for the benefit of the passengers) that should be taken is liability insurance. It is important to know, however, that the dive-boat insurance provided by PADI, in combination with crew members' professional liability insurance, covers diver passengers while in the water and on the boat. It must be emphasized that this type of insurance coverage is far more preferable a protection than merely hoping that an underwater dive-boat charter accident will not result in dive-boat liability.

Epilogue

Legal liability should not be feared as some sort of inevitable fate lurking beyond control. The concepts discussed in this manual should help the instructor, retailer, repairer, renter and boat charterer to realize that liability is the result of carelessness and lack of foresight. These factors are controllable, and hopefully, it is evident that liability can indeed be minimized with proper planning, awareness and anticipation.

Given the substantial numbers of scuba students and the amount of scuba equipment purchased and leased, the incidence of injury in recreational scuba diving is quite low. Thus, the probability of the occurrence of a liability situation is somewhat minimal, although scuba diving does contain the potential of serious injury if an accident occurs. Proper instructor conduct not only minimizes the liability risk, but can also control an accident

occurrence and thereby ensure that any initial injury doe
not become worsened.

The instructor should also have gained some insight
into the value of the association with the national certifying agency. In providing an instructor with certification
standards and student documentation, PADI has indicate
a standard of conduct based on research, experience and
legal input that provides the instructor with a reliable instructional course designed to provide for competent instruction, effective learning and student safety. The instructor may rely on PADI for the soundness of the cours
conduct. By closely adhering to certification standards, a
instructor has greatly reduced liability concerns and may
rely on the national organization's expertise in formulat-
ing these standards.

The intent of the information contained within this
manual is to prompt instructors and other scuba-industry
providers to take pause and think about their conduct.
The law of negligence liability is concerned with the consequences of unintentional acts. With all the responsibilities inherent in teaching scuba, an instructor may lose
sight of the importance of awareness and foresight. Yet,
some careful thought about conduct will go a long way in
minimizing potential accident situations. Student safety
will not result merely from making assumptions. Care and
planning must be applied to every aspect of instruction.
An instructor should continually question whether furthe
reasonable precautions are appropriate in any given situa
tion. This constant analysis of conduct may yield surprisingly effective results. An instructor should never assume
that self-protection concerns cease once the first scuba
course begins.

In its simplest form, principles of liability merely require the exercise of care, common sense, precautions,

awareness and foresight. These qualities are possessed by every instructor, but it takes some thought and self-discipline to exercise them. This is a small price to pay for the security and satisfaction of a well-taught, safe course of scuba instruction. If this information has caused some further thought and assessment of conduct, then our discussion of these legal principles has proved worthwhile.

Index

Standards, 79-81
   training, 79
   certification, 79
   deviating from, 79-80
   duty and adherence to, 32, 35, 37
   exceeding, 79
Student Records, 96-97

T

Torts, 17
Training Standards. *See* Standards.

U

Unreasonable Risk. *See* Risk.

V

Voir Dire, 56

W

Warranties. *See* Insurance.
Workmen's Compensation, 155-161
Wrongful Death, 44

Product No. 70197